SO, YOU WANN

COMIC BOOK ARTIST?

Written by Philip Amara
Illustrated by Pop Mhan

BEYOND
WORDS
Publishing
I N C

Published by
Beyond Words Publishing, Inc.
20827 NW Cornell Road, Suite 500
Hillsboro, Oregon 97124
503-531-8700/1-800-284-9673

ISBN: 1-58270-058-3

Cover Color: Guy Major
Cover and Interior Design: Amy Arendts
Editors: Barbara Mann, Carol Grimes, Leia Carlton, Kristen Schjoll, Sarah
Gabert, Claire Nunez

Printed in the United States of America
Distributed to the book trade by Publishers Group West

Library of Congress Cataloging-in-Publication Data

Amara, Philip.
    So, you wanna be a comic book artist? / written by Philip Amara ; illus-
trated by Pop Mhan.
        p. cm
    Summary: Explains to readers how to create their own superheroes,
write their own storylines, and get their comics published.
        ISBN 1-58270-058-3 (soft)
        1. Comic books, strips, etc.—Authorship. 2. Comic books, strips, etc.—
Technique. [1. Cartoons and comics—Authorship. 2. Drawing—
Technique.] I. Mhan, Pop, ill. II. Title.

PN6710 .A59 2001
808'.066741—dc21   2001035452

The corporate mission of Beyond Words Publishing, Inc.:
Inspire to Integrity

Table of Contents

INTRODUCTION

If you're a lifelong comics fan like me, you already know that one-of-a-kind feeling you get when you walk into a comic book store on the day crisp new comics are on the shelves. As a kid, I spent my Saturdays at Million Year Picnic in Boston, one of the hippest comic stores around. There, I quickly dropped large portions of my allowance on *Spider-Man*, *X-Men*, *Batman*, and later, *Flaming Carrot*, *Swamp Thing*, *Ronin*, and tons more!

By the time I was in college, I was writing articles about my favorite comics for *Comics Scene, Comics Buyers' Guide,* and for local newspapers. I even started a comics radio show and interviewed famous comics creators such as Mike Mignola of *Hellboy* and the late Jack Kirby, one of the founding fathers of Marvel Comics. Eventually, my love for comics led to a career as a creator, writer, and editor for Dark Horse. It's an incredible job—I get to create new comics every single day!

Many comics fans dream of becoming comic book artists and creators. But *how* do you do that? In your hands is a comprehensive guide to creating your own comics. It's designed to cover a variety of interests and abilities. Each chapter is packed with essential information to help you become a successful comic book artist. You'll read advice from comics greats like Bruce Timm, producer and artist of *Batman: The Animated Series*; Chris Bachalo, artist of the popular *Steampunk* comic; and *Powerpuff Girls* comic book artist, Stephanie Gladden. In addition, kid comic book artists will give their tips to help you create your own comics and publish your work. The nice thing is this book is structured so you can jump around from tools, artist tips, to whatever catches your interest!

Hi! I'm a chibi. These creatures are sometimes called *chibis*, which means "tiny" in Japanese. Chibis are this book's guides to important tips, valuable information, and comic book trivia. If you ever need to jog your memory on a certain fact, go back and look for the chibis—they'll help you out.

Whether you're starting out or have been drawing comics for years, remember this: *Anyone* can create comics if they have the inspiration and desire. You don't have to wait until you're older—there are lots of kids already creating their own comics, as you'll soon see. You can always use your comics to comment on who you are and what the world around you is like. Something as simple as comics can be pretty powerful. Only *you* can tell your story *your* way. —Phil

CHAPTER 1

So, You Wanna Be a Comic Book Artist?

You are sitting at your very own table at a comics convention. Behind you is a huge sign with your name written across it. Everything is quiet and slow. Suddenly, CRAAACK, the doors at the end of the hall burst open and a huge crowd of people rush in . . . straight toward you. They all want you to sign the latest copy of your comic book creation. Some of them are even dressed up as your characters!

"Wow," you think as you whip out your pen and begin signing, "This is surreal, man."

Have you ever imagined creating your *own* comic? With just a few tools and materials, a little guidance, and an unbridled creativity, you can! As a comics creator, the only limit is your imagination.

Every year, I attend comic book conventions where I review the work of young artists who are just starting out in comics. The one thing that they all have in common is their love for comics. Actors love acting *before* they're in a blockbuster movie or on the cover of *Entertainment Weekly*. Michael Jordan loved basketball *before* he became an NBA superstar. If you love comics, then you can potentially make money at it—even make it your career!

Comics: A Work of Art?

Your parents want to throw your comics in the trash, but you guard them with your life and make your friends swear to keep them in mint condition whenever they borrow them. Sound familiar? As with all forms of art, comics are looked at in different ways by different kinds of people. Some people consider comics to be a low form of art. Others pay lots of money to collect early editions of popular comics. It all depends on how you look at it.

Art historians often classify comics as "pop art" (short for popular art). Pop art is found everywhere in modern culture and mass media: in computer-rendered art for video games, cartoons, Japanese animated movies (anime), magazine illustrations, comic strips, and advertisements.

Did you ever think that you could change the world with a comic book? Just because comics are considered pop art doesn't mean that you can't make a serious statement with them. Some comics are so good that you could defend them as fine art or literature! Judd Winick's *Pedro and Me* and Art Spiegelman's *Maus: A Survivor's Tale* both won the Pulitzer Prize, a *very* prestigious literary award. Countless other comic book artists have been recognized and awarded for their outstanding illustrations and storytelling skills. Comics have their own language, just like music or film, for conveying emotion, message, style, and story. They can be powerful and complex, or fun and completely silly. Either way, comics always have the ability to influence the way people think.

If you're going to be a comic book artist, it's important to know that comic books are a form of sequential art.

> Sequential art is a series of repetitious drawings of characters that are used to tell a story.

This definition includes graphic novels, manga (Japanese comic books), and comic strips. In this book, I'll often refer to all these forms of "sequential art" as comics, but it's helpful to understand some differences between them. You probably already know the differences, but we've included them anyway just in case you want to wow your friends when you rattle off these fancy definitions!

Comic books: You know what they are—*Superman,* the *Fantastic Four, Tomb Raider,* and tons more! But if you want to get technical, comic books come in every kind of style and format you can imagine. Traditional comic books are usually twenty-two to thirty-two pages long and about 6 1/2 inches wide by 10 1/2 inches high, but this can vary a little . . . or a lot. Some comic books are big, oversized magazines, while others are tiny and more horizontal. Chris Ware, creator of *Acme Novelty Library,* publishes comics in all these different formats.

Comic strips: You read them every weekend in the newspaper—they're usually just a few panels long, in a horizontal format, and tell a quick story or joke. Some famous comic strips are *Calvin and Hobbes, Peanuts,* and *Bloom County.* Every once in a while, comic strips are just one panel, like *The Farside* or *Family Circus.* Years ago, comic strips like *Little Nemo in Slumberland, Prince Valiant,* and *Tarzan* took up a whole page in the newspaper!

Graphic novels: Like a book, but way better! Comics close to or over 100 pages are called graphic novels or trade paperbacks. Often, graphic novels focus on one amazingly detailed story. Some fantastic graphic novels are *Good-bye, Chunky Rice; Jar of Fools; Illegal Alien;* and *Contract with God.*

Manga comics: Literally translated, manga means "comic" in Japanese. Manga characters are sometimes magical creatures, superheroes, or ordinary kids off on a great adventure. Manga often contains themes that relate to everyday life. For example, spending long hours at school or at work is a big part of Japanese culture, and these topics are often portrayed in manga. Some of the most popular manga comics are *Sailor Moon, Ramna 1/2, Oh My Goddess,* and *Pokemon.*

Cooking Up a Killer Comic

Making a good comic is like making a tasty pizza: There are a few essential ingredients and each one has a specific role. What's a pizza without cheese, crust, and sauce? Like your favorite pizza, comics have certain key ingredients that make them comics: panels, balloons, and captions, to name a few. If you mix all these ingredients together in the right balance, you'll end up with an intriguing comic. If you leave out one or two of the major ingredients, it will show in the final product. The basic ingredients for a killer comic go a little something like this.

COMICS RECIPE

Title

Balloon

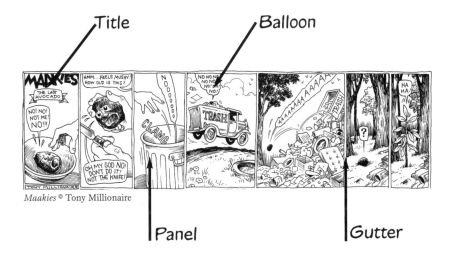

Panel

Gutter

Maakies © Tony Millionaire

Panels: Panels are the blocks of art in a comic that give your story structure. Each panel shows some kind of progression in your story, making the comic sequential. Panels can be of any size or shape as long as the art fits inside. Often, there are about six panels per page. Though you don't *have* to use panels to tell a comics story, most comic book illustrators use them to distinguish one scene from the next. Craig Thompson, who draws comics for *Nickelodeon Magazine*, sometimes draws comics without panels, or with odd-shaped panels.

Gutters: The gutters are the white margin around the page's edge and the white space between the panels. Usually panels don't butt up right against each other or go right to the edge of the page. When they do, it's called a "bleed."

Balloons: Not hot-air balloons. Not birthday balloons. Word balloons illustrate characters' conversations, loud noises, and thoughts. Comics artists usually keep the number of words per balloon small—twenty-five to forty.

Captions: Captions are like balloons. They help tell the story, but they usually do not illustrate conversation between characters. They are rectangular or square in shape and typically hold a narrator's words, describe a scene, or establish a time period in the comic.

Title: The title is what you're going to call your comic. *Ghost Rider, Young Justice, The Nevermen,* and *Spawn* are a few of the jazzy titles people have created for their comics. A snappy title that really hints at what your comic is about is important. Many people title their comics after a main character (like *Superman*) or a group of characters (like *X-Men* or the *Fantastic Four*). Your comic book title can appear anywhere on the cover, but it's usually in the top-third portion, or *tier,* of the page.

The x factor: There's one more ingredient you'll need to create an extraordinary comic: IMAGINATION. It's the *x* factor, the magic *you* bring to a story, that's going to make it memorable. What makes *Star Wars* or *The Matrix* so amazing? It's not just the special effects or the actors, but the *auteur* behind the movie—the person with a deliberate and creative vision. You're going to be the auteur behind your comic. How you execute your story and work with the above ingredients is what's going to set your comic apart!

The World of Comics Awaits You!

Okay, you've decided that you enjoy reading manga or superhero comic books so much that you want to create some of your own. You have dozens of ideas for characters and stories bubbling in your head and have started to doodle or sketch some of these characters on scraps of paper. This is just the beginning! You're about to start your own studio, learn about the tools of the trade, and get some important hints for creating your stories. You're entering the exciting world of comics!

The first issue of *Superman*, which came out in 1939, is currently worth $150,000!

Comics Creator—Kevin Eastman

Kevin Eastman's first published work appeared in one of Clay Geerdes's mini-comics, called *Clay Geerdes's Comix Wave.* At twenty-one, Kevin cocreated the hit comic *Teenage Mutant Ninja Turtles.* Currently, Kevin is working on *Ghettopolis,* a 1,000-page graphic novel with color and black-and-white pages.

When did you first start reading comics? I was six or seven when I started reading them. I had a job as a paperboy, which gave me money to buy them, and I used to trade them with pals at school (which is where I first started drawing them).

What's your favorite comic book? Lots of different ones, and for lots of different reasons. Some I like to just look at because the writing isn't so good. With some the writing is great, but I don't care for the art. Others I like for the characters, even when the writing and art are bad. My all-time favorites are Jack Kirby's *Kamandi,* Frank Miller's *Ronin,* and anything by Richard Corben—all of the above for personal and inspirational reasons. More recently, I loved *The Long Halloween* and *A Superman for All Seasons.*

When was your first professional job? I was first published by Clay Geerdes, in one of his mini-comics called *Clay Geerdes's Comix Wave.* I believe it was a three-page story that Clay paid me a dollar a page for. It was a moment in my life I will never, ever forget.

What tools of the trade do you use? Anything and everything, really—ballpoint pens and markers of every shape, form, and color—but mostly Sharpies for black line work, fine-line Staedtler's for little black details, and Pentels for white work. I destroy brushes in two sittings, so I buy cheap ones. After watching artists like Simon Bisley and Bill Sienkiewicz use anything and everything around them to create a final piece, I decided to try to never limit myself. No computer used yet, but I want to learn.

Any beginning artist tips?
I have three:

1. To tell a comic story, you have to be able to draw everything you've ever seen. Practice drawing everything from life, and draw a lot. (If you needed to draw a panel of you reading this, you'd have to draw everything you see around you right now and in some kind of perspective.)

2. Look at the artists you like and copy them—you will eventually develop and create your own vision and style of telling stories.

3. Look at your favorite film directors and study the characters, lighting, angles, and timing they choose. Try everything they try, and this will also help develop your overall personal style.

Artwork © Kevin Eastman

15

CHAPTER 2

Starting a Studio and the Tools of the Trade

You are trying to draw an incredible alien character that just popped into your head but your Bic pen just isn't doing the trick and some stale, leftover popcorn keeps rolling onto the paper, making everything greasy and gross.

"Aaargh," you yell and crumple up your drawing, throwing it on the floor. You look around your room at the mess. You just can't seem to draw anything in this trashy environment!

If you're going to be a comic book artist, you will need artist supplies that support your imagination and creativity. This chapter contains all the information you need to set yourself up to create fantastic comics.

Your Studio—Keep Out!

Before you do any drawing, writing, sketching, or inking, you'll need to put together a studio, a place where you can do your best work. Your studio doesn't have to be a private study lined with books, or an artist's loft . . . you can transform a section of your room, or turn a tabletop into a working studio.

The first step to creating your own studio is to find a space that offers some privacy, and where you feel comfortable drawing. Be sure to let your family know that this is your private work area and, if possible, not to disturb you while you're there. Once you've established an ideal location for your studio, check to make sure you have these crucial studio items.

Drawing table or desk: One of the most important features of your studio should be a good place to draw. Any kind of flat, sturdy surface will do: a card table, TV tray, kitchen table (you might want to wipe it off first), countertop, desk, or folding table. You can even buy semiportable drawing boards at an art supply store, or make one with a piece of plywood. Try to avoid drawing while lying down on the floor—it won't give your arm a proper range of motion.

Artistic supplies: Every comics artist uses different artistic supplies, but some standards include pens, brushes, and paper. See the "Tools of the Trade" section of this chapter for more information on the supplies you'll need.

Light: If your studio has a window, that's great, but a table lamp or two with bulbs of at least 75 watts are essential so that you can see well for detailed drawing and inking. At some point, you might want to invest in a Luxo-style swiveling desk lamp.

A comfy chair: Finding a chair with good back support is extremely important. With a comfortable chair, you can withstand hours of drawing comics. A cushion or pillow on the chair's seat will help as well.

Snacks: (optional) Snacks can be great while working and can energize your creativity. When you need some extra inspiration, a cookie or a banana can go a long way! Just be sure any snacks are a safe distance from your most prized artwork.

Tunes: (optional) Music can help you focus or even stimulate the creative process. You can listen to hip-hop, country, classical music (yeah, right! but it *is* supposed to help you concentrate)—whatever music *you* like to get your creative juices flowing.

Decorations: (optional) Posters by your favorite artists or pages from your favorite comics hung on the walls of your studio can help motivate your creativity.

Studio name: Give your studio a name that expresses your own unique style, for example, "Top Dog Studio," "Big, Bad Monster," or "Radical Brain Unlimited." If your studio name is "Top Dog," draw a styli-looking dog for your logo. Make a studio sign and hang it on your door or put it near your drawing table whenever you're working. Now you're in business!

WARNING: Be careful not to turn your studio into a game room: no TV, video games, dartboard, frozen pizzas, or nachos, dripping with cheese. This is not a hang-out. This is your oasis for creating your own comics—embrace its productive atmosphere!

One studio, to go! If you go away on vacation and you want to draw, make up a portable version of your studio. Put pens, pencils, and a sketchbook in a box (old lunch boxes from thrift stores work great) or a plastic zip-lock bag, so your work will be protected from the elements. You can also pack a hard, but lightweight, drawing surface if you think you'll need one.

The most important aspect of your studio is having fun while you're there. Unlike homework or chores, with drawing comics, you have the freedom to do as little or as much as you want, whenever you want. Your success is totally up to you. But remember: Success takes time and dedication, so it's also important to develop good drawing habits.

Start by going to your studio every other day for just ten to fifteen minutes. Chances are, you'll have so much fun drawing that you'll stay there longer anyway. When you're ready, try to devote more time to drawing daily, maybe forty-five minutes to an hour. Before you know it, that hour will go by as quickly as the very first fifteen minutes!

Tools of the Trade

If you really want to create great comics, you're going to require some basic drawing tools and supplies. You don't need to buy fancy art supplies—a few pencils, some pens, and an artist sketchpad will work great. You're here to draw and create, not to worry about using some superpen, forged from a mysterious asteroid. Let's face it, if you really had to, you could draw with the burnt end of a stick. The tools are important, but not as much as the ideas in your head and your willingness to express them.

Any good art store will provide one-stop shopping for pens, brushes, paper, and pencils. You might want to check out the following items once you're there.

Paper

The first sketchbook I bought was expensive, had a nice binding and a thick cover . . . and I was terrified to use it! I thought everything I sketched in it had to be good enough for a museum. When I finally tried drawing on a cheap block of newsprint, I couldn't fill it fast enough, and I got better much faster. The list below offers some helpful tips on how to find the best paper for your drawing desires.

In Japan, they use more paper for comics than they use for toliet paper!

Paper weight: Most papers come in different weights— 20 lb., 30 lb., and 50 lb. This doesn't mean that one sheet of paper weighs 100 lb. (yikes!)—the weight refers to how much a box of that particular paper weighs. Heavier paper is usually labeled 50 lb. or more. If you're sketching, light paper, like newsprint, is probably the best. But if you're producing finished art, you may want to use thicker paper that weighs more.

Newsprint: Small newsprint sketchpads work great for getting any initial ideas down on paper. You don't even have to go to an art supply store to get one. They're usually available in the stationery aisle of your supermarket. Try a 100-sheet pad of 6 x 9 inch recycled newsprint, for both pencil and charcoal drawings. They come in 9 x 12 inch sizes too, at the local art store.

Sketchpad: If you're using pencils and charcoal a lot, you might want to look into a sketchpad. Try a 100-sheet pad of 50 lb., 11 x 14 inch recycled paper. It has a slightly rough surface and is more durable than newsprint.

Drawing pad: Sometimes "sketch" paper is labeled "drawing" paper. The main difference is that drawing paper is heavier (80 lb.) than paper in a standard sketch-pad. Try a twenty-four-sheet pad of 14 x 17 inch Strathmore regular surface. Most are labeled "acidfree," which means they won't discolor over time like newsprint. Good acid-free brands of sketch paper are Strathmore, Aquabee, and Canson.

Bristol board: Most professional comic book artists use Bristol board, but it's not cheap ($10 for about twenty sheets)! You may want to stick to less expensive paper—a sketch-pad you can feel comfort-able filling with an explo-sion of ideas *and* that you won't have to worry about ruining because of the cost.

Floyd Gottfredson, who wrote and drew the *Mickey Mouse* newspaper strip, labored on fifteen thousand strips for over forty-five years.

Bristol board does have its advantages, however: It's durable and acid-free, and the size is proportionate to most comics pages. If you're interested in trying Bristol board, look for a twenty-sheet pad of 11 x 14 inch Strathmore, 100 lb. Bristol board with a smooth finish. Smooth Bristol is what most comics artists prefer because the ink works well with the surface. Coarse Bristol (also called vellum) works well for dry media, like soft pencils and charcoal, but you can ink on it, too.

Pens, Pencils, and Toothbrushes?!

Even unexpected things, like an old toothbrush, can be transformed into drawing tools. Many professional comics artists not only use typical tools like pencils, pens, and brushes but also use unorthodox—often weird—tools, too. These tools offer different levels of flexibility, reliability, and effect.

As you try these different tools, it's a good idea to experiment and see what works best for you. Keep in mind that not all experiments yield good results! Tony Millionaire, creator of *Sock Monkey,* says, "Once, I lost my favorite pen and had to do an illustration with a black Bic. It was pretty bad." Check out this list of tools, both traditional and odd, that you can find anywhere—from your bathroom cabinet to the art supply store!

Comics Creator—Stephanie Gladden

Stephanie Gladden is the creator of the comic book *Hopster's Tracks*, has been an artist for the *Powerpuff Girls* comics, and she has contributed to the *Action Girl* comics anthology series. She currently works for the Cartoon Network, one of the coolest jobs on the planet.

When did you first start reading comics? I've been reading comics ever since I was a kid. I often read comic strip collections rather than actual comic books. Some of my favorite strip collections were *Peanuts, B.C.*, and *Tumbleweeds.* I got into comic books later on while I was attending college, reading *Critters, TMNT*, and *Neat Stuff,* to name a few.

When was your first professional job? My first professional job was as an animator for an Atlanta company, doing laser shows of all things! I was twenty-one. Fortunately, I was encouraged to try illustrating comic books. It took awhile and quite a few submissions, but I eventually was given a penciling job on the *Tiny Toons* comic for DC.

What tools of the trade do you use? My favorite board is Strathmore acid-free Bristol. I prefer the 300 series with a vellum finish. I used to use a wide variety of brushes and pen nibs, but now, I've settled on the Sakura Pigma brush pen for organic lines and Pigma Micron pens for both fine-line work and straight lines.

What was the biggest professional influence on your work? *Tom and Jerry* cartoons were my biggest subconscious influence.

Any other advice for a young artist that you wish someone had told you? Learn the basics! I could have saved myself a lot of blood, sweat, and tears if I had learned drawing fundamentals such as anatomy and perspective when I was in my teens. Those things simply are not being taught in many art schools anymore.

Hopster's Tracks © Stephanie Gladden

Pencils: Okay . . . everybody knows about pencils, but not all pencils are good for drawing. A standard No. 2 pencil will work for penciling your comics, but you might want to try professional art pencils, as well.

Art pencils come in different degrees of hard and soft leads, so test them out and see what you like. An "H" on the pencil means the lead is hard, so the pencil will produce a tight, light line and will give you greater detail. A "B" on a pencil means that the lead is soft, so the pencil will produce a darker line and will create better shading effects. The higher the number on the pencil, the softer or harder the lead (8B is really soft; 6H is really hard). An "HB" means it has a good balance of both—*Sky Ape* artist Richard Jenkins opts for the HB.

Colored pencils: If you'd like to produce color comics for fun, a set of twelve to twenty-four soft, lead-centered colored pencils is wonderful to have. Colored pencils are easier to control and use than paint or colored inks. Prismacolor makes several different sets, but shop around and see what suits your needs best.

Blue pencils: Artists like Bruce Timm *(Batman Adventures)* and Brian O'Connell *(Aliens vs. Predator)* use light-blue pencils to first sketch out their drawings. They then ink over them with a brush, Pigma pen, or crow quill. The blue pencil helps provide a good guide for the ink and won't show up when you make copies of your inked pages on a copy machine.

Brushes: An excellent brush for inking is the Winsor & Newton Series 7 No. 3, for use with black India ink. But again, try different ones and see what you like. Ideally, look for a round, sable-head brush. A round-head brush gives you more versatility than a flat-head brush. Sable brushes hold ink well and won't splay after repeated cleaning and use. They range in size from 9, the largest, to 000, the smallest. The Winsor & Newton Series 7 is an excellent brush, but expensive. Check out the "Resources" section at the back of this book for more direction on using brushes, and get ready to experiment like crazy!

Crow quills: A crow quill is a versatile tool that you can use when inking your comics. Crow quills are like calligraphy pens: You dip them in ink, like a brush. They have a rigid head and combine the stiffness of a pen with the varied line weight you get from a brush.

India ink: Brushes and crow quills both use India ink. It's not a brand name; it just means it's the blackest ink you can get. Typically, comics are inked with black India ink, but feel free to experiment with other colors. India ink is permanent and waterproof, although you should still avoid getting your pages wet. Even though you can't erase India ink, you can use white-out to cover any mistakes. The ink takes at least two or three minutes to dry (watch out for smudges in the meantime!). Some good brands to keep an eye out for are Pelican and Higgins Black Magic. India ink usually comes in a glass or plastic jar, which you can dip your brush right into.

Charcoal sticks: Charcoal sticks can be messy and may take some getting used to, but once you master them, they produce a line that seems to breathe a bit more than ink (although most comics pages are inked). Charcoal is fantastic for sketching and working out your ideas on paper. Try a Ritmo charcoal pencil from Italy—it's less messy than a typical charcoal stick and gives you greater range.

Magic markers: If you're not ready for black India ink just yet, you can also use a magic marker to ink over your penciled illustrations. Unfortunately, magic

SpyBoy artist Pop Mhan sometimes likes to experiment with Q-Tips when inking his comics. Q-Tips can create a nice smooth, flat effect without the texture of a brush.

28

markers don't give you as varied a line as a brush, but they're fun and a great complementary tool to master.

Pigma pens: Pigma pens have ink in them like a marker, but a flexible head like a brush to give you varied line weight. Sakura and Pentel make really nice waterproof Pigma pens that come in several different sizes and colors.

Rulers: Rulers can be helpful for drawing panels and laying out your comic. A standard 12-inch ruler should work well for any measurements you'll need to make. Though, as an exercise, try to draw straight lines without one when you can.

White-out: Inking your comics can be tricky, so you might want to use some white-out for any corrections you may need to make when you ink. Use it with a small brush, as if it were regular ink, and carefully dab it wherever needed.

Did you notice I didn't put "eraser" on the list? I suggest not using one, especially when sketching. At this stage, there are no mistakes! You're still learning, so don't erase anything, even if you think a drawing doesn't look right. It's much better to draw that same thing again. You'll be surprised how fast you improve if you avoid using erasers while drawing.

Your tools and studio are about individual style and preference, and everyone's style and inspiration is totally different. Every artist has his or her own choice of paper, pens, pencils, and brushes. Certain artists swear by certain tools. Others use just about anything under the sun, depending on the effect they're trying to achieve. How you use these tools to perfect your illustration technique will reflect your own personal flair and comic book style.

Soon you'll be using the same kind of pens, pencils, brushes, and paper that your favorite artists use to create comics masterpieces. But, don't worry about dropping a lot of money on these items. Right now, you can use the pencils, markers, and pens that you already have lying around the house. The most important thing is to draw as much as possible and let your imagination go wild!

YOUNG ARTIST PROFILE

Ronnie Orlando, age 9

Ronnie Orlando has been drawing since he was five or six years old. His preferred drawing tools are colored pencils, which Ronnie believes add realism to his illustrations. Ronnie's favorite original character is a bird-like creature named Mighty Z, who flies throughout space, fighting crime.

Why do you want to be a comic book artist?

I want to be a comic book artist because I love to draw. I like to design my own different characters. I like all parts of drawing. Ideas just pop into my head; I draw as I go along. I like to see the finished product and see what my feelings have drawn on the paper. I like everything about drawing comics!

What is your favorite tool to use when drawing?

My favorite tools to use for drawing are colored pencils. They make the characters bright and colorful, and make them look more realistic. I like to use gel pens too—they make the pictures look really cool!

Who is Mighty Z, and how did you come up with him?

I was just drawing one day and made an eye on the paper, and suddenly the idea popped into my head to draw a bird. So then I made a beak, and I just kept drawing, and suddenly I had Mighty Z! Mighty Z flies around space and fights crime. He's from the planet Moz, and he always saves the day!

What are your plans for the future?

Drawing and making movies for a company like Disney might be fun. I have lots of drawings that I've done, but I like to draw birds the best.

What are your favorite comic books?

I really like *Star Wars* and I have a huge collection of *Star Wars* comics. My favorite character in them is R2-D2.

CHAPTER 3

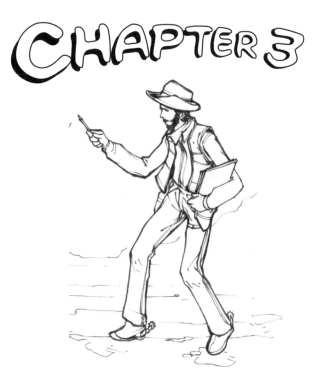

Draw, Partner!
Illustration Tips and Tricks

Drawing may be one of the most challenging aspects of creating your own comics, but with a little practice and a few tips, you can create awesome illustrations in no time! Now that you have your studio set up and own a few tools, the next step is to get your ideas down on paper.

Doodle Your Brains Out

As far as your ideas go, you're not going to remember every brainstorm you have. WRITE THEM DOWN. If you come up with an outstanding new character—a superhero, a zombie, a robot from the twenty-third century—you'll want to sketch it out, even if your idea completely changes later on.

Whatever your ideas, don't let people tell you "that's a stupid idea." Ben Edlund had an idea for a square-jawed, beefy, clueless superhero called "The Tick," whose battle cry was "Spoon!" People thought he was crazy . . . who would be interested in a superhero that wasn't so "super"? But his comic was a hit! Ben's story goes to show you that the most ingenious ideas are sometimes rejected at first.

The best way to keep track of your ideas is with an idea journal. An idea journal is your creative playground for brainstorming new ideas and sketches. It can help you flesh out your stories and characters. When you need a jolt of creativity, your journal can act as a file cabinet for your best ideas. Got an idea for a mysterious detective who stalks vampires? Make a few doodles in your idea journal of what he and the vampires look like. Jot down some notes on what the first story might be about and where it takes place.

Put your notes and your sketches on the same page, and don't move on to the next page until the first is filled up. An idea journal is not about being neat or orderly—it's about letting your imagination run rampant! Also, make sure you keep ALL of the drawings you create. You never know when you might need to look back and find some extra inspiration.

Sketched Out!

Sketching is the most important thing you can do right now to improve your skills as an artist. The very first comics you ever draw are going to look rough—they're *supposed* to look that way! Don't get discouraged. Every comic book artist begins with messy, unrefined, even sloppy, sketches of their comics. Have fun with your illustrations, and don't worry about making anything look perfect. Sketching is about getting your ideas down on paper, practicing your drawing skills, and working out your character's looks and style—your sketches are for *you*, to help you improve as an artist.

Try to sketch as often as possible. Remember, established comics artists have spent years perfecting their drawing techniques. No matter what age they started creating comics, I guarantee that they all drew hundreds of sketches before they even thought of being published. They sketched tons of things from real life *and* things from their imagination. And that's what you're going to do too!

Sketching Exercises

Ugly, attractive, weird, goofy-looking, hefty, muscle-built, slender, and stocky are just a few of the zany qualities you can give your comic book characters. What makes an expression on a face happy, sad, or angry? The following tips will help you bring your comic book characters to life!

Get sticky: You can sketch stick figures and show them running, sitting, sleeping, or jumping. Then use those figures as skeletons or guides for more detailed characters, like jittery robots, talking salamanders, sly monkeys that steal top hats, and even regular people.

Action shots: Once you've sketched your character, try drawing it from several different angles—side views, top views, action shots, and close-ups. Keep these sketches as a guide sheet for creating future illustrations.

Quick 'n' easy comic strip: Choose one of your favorite three-panel comic strips from the weekly newspaper, such as *Garfield, Mutts, Over the Hedge,* or *Calvin and Hobbes.* On a piece of sketch paper, draw the strip. Don't trace and don't worry about copying the artist's style to perfection. Next, draw a second strip, this time replacing the comic strip characters with ones of your own. By following the work of professional comics artists, you can learn from their composition and style.

Exaggerate: Begin by drawing an ordinary face, either male or female, and then exaggerate and distort different

Comics Creator—Craig Thompson

Craig Thompson is the award-winning creator of *Good-bye, Chunky Rice* and the forthcoming *Blankets* graphic novel. At twenty-two, he landed his first professional comics job for Dark Horse's *Scatterbrain* anthology and now often draws strips for *Nickelodeon Magazine*.

What inspires you? Real life always stirs up the best inspiration. My newest book focuses on the experience of growing up in rural Wisconsin with my little brother—our family, our fights, our playtime—and the countryside we explored—forests, streams, and snow-covered winters. Comics can be fantastic stories with spaceships and monsters you make up in your imagination, or they can be about simple things like going to school or the grocery store, or swimming at the lake in summer.

Any beginning-artist tips? Draw comics. It's the best thing you can do to break into the industry. Before worrying about "being noticed" or making money, just draw your own stories—draw whatever you want and draw a lot.

What's the coolest thing about being a comics artist?
Having something to show for your time. Looking back over a year and having actual pages drawn to measure your personal and creative growth.

Any other advice for young artists? "Cartoonist" is a label you give yourself, not a title validated by your notoriety or the amount of money you make cartooning. The first step toward becoming a cartoonist is declaring yourself one. This same ethic applies to tools. Fancy brushes and paper and desks don't make one a cartoonist. Drawing cartoons does. One of my favorite cartoonists, Ronald Searle, drew some of his best works while imprisoned in a concentration camp. He didn't have any fancy tools there, only the constant threat of disease and torture.

Are you a self-taught artist, or did you go to art school?
Self-taught, though I attended art school for one semester and community college for one year. Of the two, college was far less expensive and far more useful. I'd recommend young cartoonists to pursue a balanced education with science, history, and literature because that knowledge will fuel plenty of ideas and enhance your cartooning vocabulary more than color wheels and wood-shop classes.

Blankets © Craig Thompson

features. What would your character look like with a monstrous forehead and blue skin? How about a long and pointy nose or gnarled teeth? There's no need to stick to realism. In fact, most comics characters have exaggerated features. The eyes and mouths are especially expressive. You can also interchange facial features to create an almost limitless variety of expressions. Manga style artist Ryan Kinnaird, creator of *Mystic Edge*, uses a variety of expressions to give his comics punch!

Enraged

Joyful

Freaked Out

Word play: Warm up your creative juices by transforming someone else's words into images. Think of one of your favorite books or songs, and draw how you envision the setting and characters. Or randomly pick three words from the dictionary (pineapple, automobile, excited) and see if that inspires a wacky character and story!

Picture perfect: Cut out pictures from magazines that could provide inspiration for your own unique drawings. Use these items as references for your own sketches, and let your imagination wander. Build up a reference folder that you can access when you need help drawing a car, building, or body type.

Switch it up: Sketching doesn't have to be with a pencil. Try drawing the same objects with different items: pens, charcoal, markers, or paints. Notice the variety of results. You can also make up a tool of your own (like the Q-Tips or toothbrushes mentioned in Chapter 2). When you master a unique tool, it can be your secret weapon—like a deadly three-pointer in a basketball game—for making an extraordinary comic.

Funky shapes: Choose five objects of different shapes and sizes from around your house. Keep the shapes simple. Draw your five objects quickly with a pencil, then try to transform the objects into interesting characters. A balloon shape can meld into Jiggly Puff from *Pokemon*. A few cones and cylinders might morph into *Star Wars* droids. Circles, ovals, squares, and triangles can all transform into a cute San Rio-style character like Hello Kitty or Choco Kat; just follow these steps.

Step 1—Draw basic circles and ovals.

Step 2—Add facial features and other rough details.

Step 3—Tighten up the details and try giving your character a nice, thick outline.

Inking Your Sketches

Typically, comic book artists use a pencil to rough out the drawings and then ink over the pencil with a pen or brush. When you're done trying these sketching exercises, try inking over your work with a felt-tip pen or magic marker for practice before you try brushes or Crow quills. You can even do inks on tracing paper, so your pencil drawings remain untouched and you can practice inking over them as many times as you want. Don't worry about making your illustrations perfect—remember, nobody has to see these sketches but you!

What About Art School?

You don't have to go to art school to be a comics artist. Many comics artists are self-taught. But keep in mind, if you don't go to art school, you need to be the kind of person who *really* understands commitment. You must hold yourself accountable to achieve a dream, because you know the rewards are worth it.

Artists like Steve Bissette *(Swamp Thing, Tyrant)*, Marvel artists Adam and Andy Kubert, George Pratt *(Enemy Ace)*, and Paul Chadwick *(Concrete)* all went to art school. Fan favorites like Humberto Ramos *(Crimson, Out There)* and artists like Chynna Clugston-Major *(Blue Monday)* are mostly self-taught. *SpyBoy*'s Pop Mhan studied formal technical drawing but is self-taught when it comes to comics.

There are excellent art schools at the high school and college level all over the country. Some offer programs that focus specifically on drawing comics. Art school, in general, teaches you things such as anatomy, perspective, composition, color theory, and storytelling. There's no right decision on whether or not to go to art school for comics. Take some time to think about it. The good thing is, nothing's stopping you from creating comics right *now*.

A Truly Original Comic

Your journal is going to become very valuable to you, as a budding comics creator. It's almost like a diary for your story ideas and sketches. It's the place to create whatever springs into your mind, no matter how strange, wacky, or unique the idea may be. Chances are, you'll come up with a truly original comic based on these early concepts and sketches, so don't ever second-guess your creativity and imagination: Those are the things that will make your comic book shine!

YOUNG ARTIST PROFILE

Kristen Joerger, age 13

Kristen Joerger started drawing comics when she picked out a magazine at the store that had some manga in it. She became fascinated with the way the comics were drawn. She loved the stories and the artwork, so she tried it!

Why do you want to be a comic book artist?
Basically, I want to be a comic book artist because I love drawing. Drawing is a big part of comic books. I also like being creative and developing stories.

Where do you get your ideas from?
I get my ideas from pretty much anywhere! If I see something interesting, I try to draw a picture around it. Sometimes I get my ideas from other artists. I think the best way to learn is to see what others have drawn and then put your own twists on them.

What are your tools for drawing comics?
Just me, my paper, and my pencils. I don't like coloring my pictures because sometimes you can lose the meaning of the picture when you color it in.

Who is your favorite comic character to draw?
I love all the characters I draw! My fave out of all the pictures I sent in is the Japanese little girl. I like her because she is fun and happy. The outfit she is wearing is an outfit you might see on a little girl in gym class in Japan. The characters on her shirt say "Japan."

CHAPTER 4

Character Creation: From Superheroes to Villains

You rise from the old city reservoir, covered in radioactive muck. Once, you were human, but now you are superstrong and nearly invincible. Unfortunately, the poisonous goo also made you a freakish creature that terrifies everyone who crosses your path. Oh, wait . . . it's not you! It's just your comic book character!

Comic book characters can come in any shape and size, from superheroes to monsters to ordinary kids doing extraordinary things. What kind of characters do you envision for your comic book? How about a tragic mutant

like *X-Men*'s Wolverine, or a goofball like *Archie*'s
Jughead, who bumbles into mischief? Maybe your comic
is about *you*. In that case, you and your friends can
become the characters.

How you choose your character comes from the
kinds of comics you enjoy. If you like *Diablo* (the game or
the comics), then your character could be a barbarian,
necromancer, or paladin. If you are fascinated with
Japanese anime, you could model your character after
Sailor Moon, the space pirate Captain Harlock, or the girl
cops from *You're Under Arrest*.

Coming Up with a Character

There isn't one perfect set of rules for creating characters,
but there are some guidelines that can help you lay the
foundation of your character's personality, history, and
motivation. Once you know these basics, all that's left to
do is choose which of your characters to draw first!

Origin: The Kid from Krypton

As you create your character, imagine an **origin** for him
or her. Basically, origin is the place your characters come
from and how they got to be where they are now. Everybody knows the story of Superman's origin: Before the
planet Krypton explodes, a scientist named Jor-El spares
his baby son, Kal-El, by placing him safely in a rocket pod
and sending him millions of miles through space to Earth,

where the energy from our sun gives him the powers of Superman! Write down a few sentences about your character's origin.

Motivation: Behind the Mask of the Caped Crusader

Character **motivation** can explain why a character acts or reacts a certain way, and is an important part of your character's personality. Batman fights crime because, as a boy, his parents were murdered by a mugger. In the guise of Batman, the orphaned millionaire, Bruce Wayne, vows to protect the innocent people of Gotham City from a similar fate. Batman's motivation for fighting crime is his parents' death. Sometimes, a similar event can create different motivations for different characters. Bruce Wayne and Oswald Cobblepot are both orphans. One became the heroic Batman, and one chose a life of crime as the despicable villain, the Penguin.

> Superman's alter ego, Clark Kent, was created by combining the names of actors Clark Gable and Kent Douglas.

Personality: The Good, the Bad, and the Ugly

You might want to give your characters more dynamic personality traits than the "good guys" versus the "bad guys." If you limit your characters to these common traits, you may find that your comics become flat and unexciting. Try to keep your readers on their toes! Character

personality is what you'll articulate in the pages of your comic with your character's expressions, actions, and dialogue. For example, the X-men all have very different personalities.

Cyclops: Dull but brave, a consummate leader.
Colossus: Noble and selfless in the face of danger.
Wolverine: Primal, unflinching in battle, and haunted by a hazy past he's only begun to piece together.
Storm: Reserved, but emotions bubble just beneath the surface.

You can create characters that are excitable, stoic, thoughtful, spoiled, noble, or confident. As a character exercise, you can practice observing the personalities of people around you: your friends, family, and people at school or on the street. Use these personalities as models for your own characters. Pay attention to the qualities that make people unique.

Heroes Versus Villains

Heroes and villains are two of the most common character types found in comic books. Captain America was frozen during World War II and then unfrozen later to protect America against evildoers. The Red Skull, on the other hand, is a dangerous Nazi leader with plans to control the world. The former is a hero, and the latter is a villain. A

Comics Creator—Brian Ralph

Brian Ralph is the creator of the award-winning small-press comics hits, *Cave-In* and *Crum Bums*. He is a graduate of Rhode Island School of Design, where he majored in illustration.

When did you first start reading comics? I read some comics when I was little, like *Richie Rich, Hot Stuff!*, and *Casper*. I just read the same issues over and over. When I was twelve, I started to read superhero comics and trace them.

What's your favorite comic book? There are so many! Maybe it's Jack Kirby's *The Eternals*. I have so many favorites though. I love Japanese comics. I can't read the words, but I learn from the pacing and compositions. I love comics by Chris Ware; Charles Burns; Herge, the creator of *Tin-Tin*; and others. I learn little bits from each person!

When was your first professional comics job? Hmm, that's a tough question. I've always self-published my work, and I've always had a do-it-yourself attitude. I get little comics jobs here and there, but mostly I self-publish and do comics for me.

What has been the biggest professional influence on your work? I used to live in a warehouse with a lot of cartoonists and artists, complete with bats and mice. It was cold and almost like living in a dark cave. That's what motivated me to create *Cave-In*. I get inspired and influenced by my surroundings, people I meet, and things I see. I interpret them through my comics.

Any other advice for breaking into comics that you wish someone had told you? Don't be discouraged if you think you can't draw as well as someone else. So many artists get frustrated and quit. You should stick with it and realize that everyone, even the beginners, have something unique to add to the world of comics and art. If you have great stories to tell and an interesting way to develop a comic, there is always something special about what you do, so . . . don't get discouraged!

What's your best hint for the right way to start an illustration or sequential comic page/strip? Before I begin an illustration or a panel of a comic, I sketch out a "thumbnail" drawing. It doesn't have to be very big, and it can be sloppy. It's like a practice version. Sometimes it takes a few sketches before you get it right. Try a few different compositions until you are happy, and then you can use that sketch as a reference. I look at the sketch and use it to guide me when making the final drawing. When you are doing the panel, start out by drawing lightly and work the entire drawing all at once. Don't finish the character and then have no idea what the background will look like. You need to work on everything all at once. It can start out a bit sloppy; just put things in where they should go, and then slowly begin to tighten up the drawing, fixing and fiddling until you have it the way you want it.

Cave-In © Brian Ralph

49

classic hero is typically motivated to defend the less fortunate, uphold justice, show compassion, and ensure people's freedom. A classic villain can be self-serving, bloodthirsty, hateful, and manipulative. Your character doesn't have to fall into a classic hero or villain category—these are just common character types. It's great if your hero wins most of his battles, but he doesn't have to excel at every turn. Some failures will improve your character's believability and make for a more exciting adventure.

Personality Profile

Ask yourself these questions to help determine your character's personality profile.

Character profile:

Where was your character born?

What was your character's family like?

What important events made your character who he or she is today?

Superhero profile:

What kind of superpower does your character have?

How did your character get his or her amazing powers?

Does your character have a secret identity?

Action hero profile:

Does your character have a costume that hides his or her

identity? Are there any special tools, weapons, or equipment that your character uses?

Does your character have cool transportation (Batman's Batmobile for example)?

In 1961, Marvel Comics rejuvenated the comic book scene with the creation of the *Fantastic Four*, an atypical superhero group that didn't wear capes and masks, and made no attempt to keep their identity a secret.

Sidekick profile:

When and how did your sidekick meet the hero he works with?

Where does your sidekick live?

What are your sidekick's powers or special abilities?

Character Creations

Here are some ideas to get you started on your own character creations.

Make yourself the star: When creating your comic book characters, you can always use your own life as inspiration. You could do a *great* comic book simply about your life. Use an experience and lay it out in comic format. Ever wished you could change your past? This time, the outcome is all in your hands!

All in the family: Create characters out of your family members and closest friends. If your grandma had a superpower, what would it be? Maybe your mom actually does have eyes in the back of her head. Think about their strongest traits, either good or bad, and have fun playing off of them.

Alter egos: Think about a famous comic character who seems to have another side to him. Remember how Bruce Banner transforms into the Hulk whenever he's angry? Use this idea of the alter ego to create your own interesting characters from ones you already know. Does Archie Andrews have an evil twin? Is there a good version of Dr. Doom out there somewhere?

Animals: Create a story where all the characters are animals. Each animal can represent a different character personality in your story. A nasty bulldog can be the school bully, or a pesky chickadee can be a nosy neighbor. What animals could you use to create a character who's brave, sinister, or goofy?

Wonder Woman's battle cry, "Keep 'em flying," became a well-known wartime slogan, and in 1943, she was even shown leading marines into battle.

Be Inspired!

Your hero is a muscle-bound champion from a far planet. His nemesis is a villainous vampire, thawed after centuries in Arctic ice. Their battles will become the stuff of legends, and you're the one who gets to create their adventures! In comics, you can build any kind of characters you want and put them into any kind of story. You can create superheroes, be inspired by manga, invent some wacky animal char-acters, and/or create stories about ordi-nary people. The trick is to add something of yourself, on some level, to all your cre-ations. Use your experience and instincts to give them that extra punch. It'll help set your comics apart from everything else.

The first issue of *Incredible Hulk* which came out in 1962 is now worth $13,000. In that first issue, the Incredible Hulk is gray!

YOUNG ARTIST PROFILE

Adrian Rima, age 13

Adrian Rima has known that he wanted to be a comic book artist since he was four years old. His favorite comics include *Sonic and Knuckles*, *Gundam Wing*, and *Dragonball Z*. Adrian's comics have been displayed in galleries and recognized in his school's drawing contest. According to Adrian, the most important thing for other comics artists to do is to never give up on drawing.

Why do you want to be a comic book artist?
I've always wanted to draw professionally. I draw every day. I share my artwork with my friends and teachers. Sometimes my schoolmates want to buy my pictures.

What cool things have you done to get your comics noticed?

I drew caricatures of everyone in my sixth grade class, which were published in our yearbook. I also drew caricatures of some of the people in my acting class, including the director, and shared them. One of my comic pictures is on display at the Art and Clay Studio gallery. I was also in a drawing contest at school and received a plaque with my name on it.

What are your favorite comics?
I like *Sonic and Knuckles* because they are cartoon animals with big heads and large eyes, with special powers like running really fast and punching really hard. I like *Gundam Wing* because robots are awesome warriors and the pilots are smart teenagers. I like *Dragonball Z* because the characters are superstrong warriors that can float and shoot energy balls.

What would you tell other kid comic book artists?
I would tell them to practice a lot and never give up on their drawings. If you are a beginner, don't quit after a few days. People tell me my drawings are

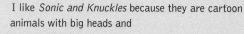

good, and that's because I've been practicing for eight years. There are many different styles of drawing, and each has its good points, so it's important not to judge your drawings. During the past school year, I was a helper for my art teacher during my recess times. I worked with kindergartners, and second and fourth graders. When they had been absent or needed extra help with their art projects, the teacher would ask me to help them. I would sit next to them and give them pointers. For instance, if a nose needed to be bigger, I would draw it on a separate paper so they could see if it was a good idea.

Where do you get your ideas?
When I feel like drawing, I just think of something I'd like to draw, and then I draw it. Sometimes I get my ideas when I'm watching a movie or TV, or reading a comic. I make it into a cartoon or other picture.

CHAPTER 5

Creating Stellar Stories: Comic Book Scripts

Now that you've started writing and sketching your character ideas in your sketchpad and idea journal, the next step is creating the world they inhabit . . . and, of course, deciding what they do there! This chapter is all about how to create action-packed stories for your comic.

Pick a Genre . . . Any Genre!

There are tons of comics out there with as many different story styles as there are readers. There are superhero comics like *Superman, Iron-Man, Spawn, WildC.A.T.S., Fathom,* and *Spider-Man*. There are non-superhero comics, too, including *Bone*, *Sock Monkey*, *Scary Godmother*, *Flood*, and *Skeleton Key*. The good thing is, there's something out there for whatever your tastes might be.

There are so many exciting genres in comics: science fiction, horror, westerns, martial arts, superheroes, real-life adventure . . . the list goes on. Think of your favorite movie, then try to figure out what genre that movie belongs to. *X-Men* would be the superhero genre. *The Matrix* would be science fiction. *The Lord of the Rings* would be sword and sorcery, or fantasy. Use that genre to inspire your comics story.

Writing the Perfect Comic Book Story

Now that you've determined what genre you would like to try, you're ready to put together a comic book story. Here are some helpful questions to ask yourself when devising the perfect tale.

Premise: What's your idea for a story?
Theme: What's the message behind the story?
Plot: What will your characters do?
Setting: Where do your characters live? In what time period?

Premise

Most comic book stories start with a premise or idea. The premise behind *Star Trek* is "to boldly go where no man has gone before." *Spider-Man*'s premise is that teenager Peter Parker is bitten by a radioactive spider and becomes a superhuman crime fighter. The story in any given issue of *Star Trek* or *Spider-Man* will deal with this premise. What will be your story's premise?

Theme

Don't worry about the prospect of adding a theme to your story. A theme doesn't need to be complex—just any subject or topic of discussion that concerns you. After all, if you're driven to create a comic, you surely have something to say about the world around you. This can be your comic book theme.

You might be surprised by some of the themes found in your favorite comics. *X-Men* comics have a message about discrimination, *Spider-Man* has the theme that with greater power comes greater responsibility, and *The Nevermen* shows that humanity can be redefined by technology. Make a list of ten issues that affect you and try turning them into a theme for your story.

Jim Davis, creator of *Garfield*, got his inspiration from his childhood—he grew up on an Indiana farm with 25 cats!

Plot

The series of events that make up your story is called the plot. Your idea journal is a great place to start jotting down bits and pieces of ideas for your story's plot: a confrontation with a villain, a mystery that needs to be solved, a journey into the unknown. For fun, try drawing your story ideas instead of writing them down. If your character comes from outer space, draw a sketch of a spaceship rocketing toward Earth. Your illustrations can tell the story as much as your words.

Story Starters

How do you start a story? You don't have to start at the beginning. Write about the parts of the story that excite you most, and build the rest of the story around your core ideas. Here are some other sweet tricks to get you goin'!

Reinvent the classics: Think of a fairy tale, fable, or myth whose ending has always driven you crazy, and rewrite it the way you think it should go, or tell it anew from a particular character's point of view. Maybe a tragedy can become a comedy or maybe the good guy doesn't always win. Maybe it's told by the guy on the street selling newspapers, instead of the hero. It's all up to you to decide.

Comics Creator—Chris Bachalo

Chris Bachalo has worked on cool comics like *Shade, The Changing Man, Generation X,* and *Sandman.* Now he helms the wild world of *Steampunk,* his own comic series!

When did you first start reading comics? When I was ten.

What's your favorite comic book? When I was a kid, my fave was *Werewolf-by-Night.* When the moon stopped rising for that title, I became enlightened by the spin-off, *Moon Knight!*

When was your first professional comics job? I was twenty-three and was handed a fill-in gig on *Sandman #12* as I waited for the script of my first regular gig, *Shade, the Changing Man,* to be completed.

What are you the current artist on/creator of? The industrial gothic, sci-fi, action adventure, love-story comic series, *Steampunk!*

Where did you go to art school? California State University, Long Beach.

What tools of the trade would you recommend? Tools of the trade that I use on a frequent basis are Staedtler Mars lead holder, Staedtler Mars HB leads, Staedtler plastic erasers, kneaded eraser, a ruler, Rotring art pens, Niji water brushes, several circle and oval templates, Umax Mirage D-16 scanner, and Photoshop on my computer.

Who was the biggest professional influence on your work?
Comics artist Michael Golden was the first guy who really inspired me—Frank Frazzetta, as well. Every good artist to one degree or another has inspired something in me.

Any beginning-artist tips?
Draw a five-page story featuring your favorite character that demonstrates that you *know* how to draw a superhero, regular people, cars, trucks, phones, trees, buildings, pizzas, and hamburgers. Draw *and* tell a story, complete with an action scene and a scene with folks sitting on a bench and having a conversation.

Any other advice for young artists? The best journey begins in the classroom. It's a great place to learn how to draw a circle, paint a painting, and design a logo. It's a sweet place to meet other buds who enjoy art, and will be the easiest "A" you'll ever get. Imagine being graded on how to make a circle! Too much fun, man!

What's the coolest thing about being a comics artist? I would say that being my own boss, working at home, and having my own hours are pretty nice perks of the biz!

Steampunk art © Chris Bachalo

News flash: Watch the news or read the newspaper and see what is going on in the world around you. Wonder Woman, one of the most patriotic superheroes ever, was created in response to World War II. Maybe you can create a story about someone who seeks to form a more peaceful world and fights terrorism. If there's an issue you have a strong opinion about, don't be afraid to voice it in your comics. They're perfect for that.

Oldies but goodies: Take a trip to a local comic book store and look at some of the old comics that have helped shape today's comics, such as the *Fantastic Four*, *Superman*, *Batman*, *X-Men*, *The Incredible Hulk*, and *Spider-Man*. What is it about these comics that makes them great? Use an event in one of these stories as a starting point for your own comic story.

Cliff-hangers

If you're writing a continuing story that will be told over several issues, you might want to add several cliff-hangers to keep your readers coming back for more! Cliff-hangers are great for building suspense. Maybe a hero is being pursued by a villain. The villain, though, turns out to be an old friend! The readers don't see that until the last page and have to wait to see how the story plays out in the next issue. Check out these other cliff-hanger ideas.

Escaped! After pages of hot pursuits, when we finally think the hero's caught the villain for good, he escapes!

Dead or alive? A main character could be left to die at the end of an issue, leaving the readers wondering whether he'll survive . . .

Matt Groening, creator of *The Simpsons*, named many of his characters after street names in his hometown of Portland, Oregon.

The clock is ticking . . . Will the hero be able to diffuse the bomb in time? Will he save the planet before it's destroyed?

True identities. So you think you finally figured out the villain's true identity? Think again!

Settings

The setting or background of your comic is where your story will take place. They can be anywhere in the universe and at any point in time, real or imagined. Most comic book stories have more than one setting. Need a good setting for your story? Here are a few ideas.

Your own backyard: There's an old saying that people know best what's in their own backyard. You can take elements from your "backyard" and weave them into a powerful imaginary setting. In *Star Wars*, Luke Skywalker is an anxious kid yearning for adventure and purpose away from his Uncle Owen's boring space farm. Instead of the setting being the fields of Nebraska or Iowa, it's the imagined sci-fi setting of Tatooine.

Mise-en-scène (meez-ahn-sahn): In film terminology, there's a fancy word, *mise-en-scène*, which means "to put in place." It's typically at the beginning of a movie, and it gives the audience an accurate, compelling look at a story's setting. For example, a mise-en-scène of a bombed-out city in post-World War II Europe would let you know that the characters are living in a bleak era in history. The mise-en-scènes in a *Samurai Jack* cartoon let you know what life is like in ancient Japan, or the bleak future under the rule of the villain, Aku. You might want to try creating a mise-en-scène to set a particular mood at the beginning of your story.

Paradise lost? Imagine a world with all of your favorite things in one place, along with all of the things that you always wished existed. What would your ideal world look like? Try the opposite of this, too. If the main character of your comic book were placed in the worst environment you could ever imagine, what would it look like?

Treasure Chest

Now that you've tried out some new ideas for creative story lines, it's important to remember one thing: DON'T THROW ANYTHING AWAY! Take a box and decorate it with paint and stickers. Or draw skulls and crossbones on it so that no one will spy on your ideas. Make it into a treasure chest of your imagination. You never know when you'll go back and use some little tidbit from one of your old stories. You might not think it's good now, but five years from now you could think it's the greatest idea ever!

YOUNG ARTIST PROFILE

David Edward Barnes, Jr., age 16

David Edward Barnes, Jr. started reading *Sonic, the Hedgehog* **comic books when he was eight years old and has since become a fan of** *Spider-Man, X-Men,* **and Marvel's new line of Ultimate comic books. Not satisfied with just reading the comics, David began drawing his own and has already gained recognition for his work, including winning three different calendar contests and his school newspaper's drawing contests.**

What are your favorite comics?
As a fan of *Sonic, the Hedgehog,* I first began buying these comics around the age of eight or so. I later progressed to the ever-famous *Spider-Man* comics and then *The X-Men.* Currently, I am interested in Marvel's new Ultimate line of comics. With over 430 comics in my collection, I consider myself a true fan.

Why did you decide to start drawing comics?
I was never satisfied with just reading these fine pieces of literature and therefore began to draw.

Have you ever taken an art class?
Aside from art class in school and one summer art program, I've never had any lessons. Drawing has always been my talent, and I hope the world may someday see my skills in print.

What have you done to get your work noticed?
I have dreamed of becoming a comic book artist and have taken several steps to get my work noticed. I entered several calendar contests and won three different

times. The first time, I won the cover, which was a $75 prize. I also entered my school newspaper's drawing contests and won two movie tickets and being printed in the paper as the prize. I have also submitted drawings to *Archie* comics and one of my *Sonic, the Hedgehog* drawings was printed in issue 47. Last, but not least, I was voted as "Most Artistic" in my eighth grade yearbook. With a dream and numerous successes with various contests, I believe I may very well achieve "comic artist" as my future occupation.

What would you tell other kid comic book artists? Look into using drawing books—they help a lot in making your artwork better. I used a book by Marvel Comics, and it helped a lot. Doodle constantly and always work at it—it's the only way you will get better.

Where do you get your ideas? Sometimes I will see a character in a comic book that will influence what I draw. Most of my ideas come from inside my head though, and I just go with whatever comes out.

What tools do you use to create your comics? A regular old No. 2 pencil works the best for me.

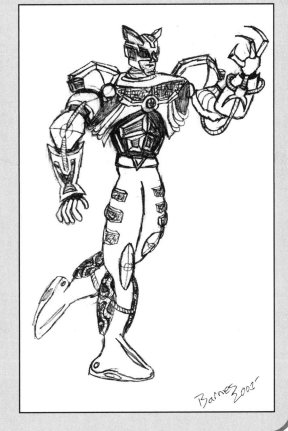

CHAPTER 6

Layout: Putting It All Together

Before you launch a full-fledged comic book, you'll need to break down your illustrations and story ideas into several steps: scripting your comic, drawing thumbnails, creating penciled pages, inking your work, creating a cover, and choosing a title.

Scripting Your Comic

Because comic book stories are told entirely through dialogue, you will need to write a script for your comic book before you illustrate it, just like you would if you were writing a play. Good dialogue should be interesting, tell you something about the characters, *and* advance the plot.

Because much of the comic book story can be told through the characters' expressions and body language, your characters' conversations can be brief and to the point. You can also use sound effects like "Zap!," "Crunch-crunch!," or "Sproing" to jazz up your story!

The following is a script excerpt from *Sky Ape: Waiting for Crime* as an example of what your script might look like. Notice the scene descriptions, dialogue, sound effects, and captions.

Sample Page from a *Sky Ape* Script

PANEL 1
SCENE DESCRIPTION: KIRK MADGE (SKY APE) IS IN AN UNDERSIZED T-SHIRT (EMBLAZONED WITH THE LEGEND, "BAY CITY ROLLERS") AND A PAIR OF GOGGLES WITH MAGNIFYING LENSES AND ALL SORTS OF DOOHICKEYS. HE HAS TOOLS IN ONE OF HIS HANDS, AS HE HOLDS HIS JETPACK WITH HIS FEET. HIS APARTMENT, WHAT WE CAN SEE ANYWAY, IS SPARSELY DECORATED.

CAPTION: DOWNTOWN BOSTON

VOICE (OFF PANEL): HEY! . . .

PANEL 2
SCENE DESCRIPTION: MEDIUM SHOT. IN THE DOORWAY TO KIRK'S APARTMENT STANDS FRANCIS BIRD. SHE IS SHAPELY, DRESSED QUITE COQUETTISHLY (JEANS AND A SHORT-SLEEVE RINGER TEE THAT HUGS HER FIGURE), AND HER HAIR IS DOWN. SHE HAS AN ATHLETIC AND SOMEWHAT MYSTERIOUS AIR ABOUT HER.

FRANCIS: . . . I THOUGHT **YOU** WERE GONNA **DO** MY TAXES.

PANEL 3
CAPTION: CLOSE-UP ON SKY APE, A.K.A, KIRK MADGE, SQUINTING OR FURROWING HIS BROW AS HE TINKERS WITH HIS OFF-PANEL JETPACK.

KIRK: CAN'T . . .

PANEL 4

CAPTION: MEDIUM SHOT. KIRK SITS ON THE FLOOR, BACK TO THE READER, AS HE CONTINUES TO WORK THE BUGS OUT OF HIS JETPACK.

KIRK: . . . IT'S JETPACK NIGHT. GOTTA TINKER WITH THIS NEW DESIGN. THE FLANGES ARE WACK, YO.

LINK: THE EXHAUST SYSTEM IS CRUNCHED, AND RUNNING THIS THING ON CHAMPAGNE IS KILLING ME!

Sketching Thumbnails

Your script is just the start. The next step is changing all your scene descriptions from text to art. To help map out your comic page, you might want to first draw some thumbnail sketches for each panel. **Thumbnails** are quick, loose sketches that you draw before you begin the penciled page. Artists use thumbnails to sketch out character positions, perspectives, and light sources *before* they draw a comics page. Thumbnails are great because you can change a panel without having to redo your whole comic from scratch. Richard Jenkins, the artist of *Sky Ape*, does detailed thumbnails and is primarily concerned with character position, as shown here:

Sky Ape Thumbnail

Artwork © Richard Jenkins

70

Ready to try some thumbnails? Using one of your completed scripts, draw a very rough, quick sketch to correspond with each panel in your script. This shouldn't take long. When you're done, you will have a set of thumbnails outlining your comic sequence.

The first comic books were sold for ten cents and were sixty-four pages long.

Drawing the Panels

Once you've finished your thumbnails, you can illustrate the penciled pages using your thumbnails as a guide. Take your time! Professional comics artists draw about one to four pages per week, on average. Between each panel, leave about a quarter of an inch of white space for the gutter. Focus on drawing your characters and setting first, then try to position balloons or captions later without covering too much art.

Inking

Inking your comics can take some time to master at first. Here's a tip: The more you practice using your brush and inking in your sketchbook, the better it will look on your comics page. Dip your brush gently into the ink bottle. You may want to try a couple of test lines on a separate piece of paper before you ink your penciled illustrations. Draw very lightly at first to get a feel for the width of the

brush. It's different from a rigid pencil, right? The more
you practice, the more you'll notice the amazing range it
will offer. Don't worry if you make a mistake . . . it's easy
to make corrections with white-out after the ink dries.
Here is an example of the same page from *Sky Ape,* in finished form.

Sky Ape Inked Page

SkyApe ™ © Amara, McCarney, Jenkins, Russo.

Designing Your Cover

The cover can be one of the most important and dynamic pieces of your comic book. There are lots of amazing comics illustrators who have designed great covers—Jack Kirby, Will Eisner, Alex Toth—you might want to look at some of their covers for inspiration. If you want a quick way to do a cover composition, try a big, expressive head shot. Or, you can show a cool action scene from your storyline. Whatever you decide to draw for the cover, make sure it's fun and intriguing enough so that people will want to pick up your comic and read it.

Kapow! You've Got a Finished Comic!

You've written an awesome script and have been drawing in your sketchbook like there's no tomorrow. Now it's time to get crackin' on your very first comic book pages. Here's a secret: Keep things loose, and don't try to perfect the pages too much. The first pages you ever do will look rough, and that's okay. Enjoy every stage of drawing the pages: the thumbnails, the pencils, the inks, the lettering, and the coloring. At this stage, a healthy, excited attitude is more important than artistic perfection. When you sit down in your studio, have a big smile on your face, and have fun creating your comic. It's one of the greatest jobs in the world!

Comics Creator—Pop Mhan

Pop Mhan is a self-taught comics artist with a technical drawing background. Pop has numerous comics credits, including *SpyBoy, Planet of the Apes, Ghost Rider, Star Wars: Jedi Quest,* and *Magic: The Gathering,* among others. Currently, he is working on the crossover comic *SpyBoy/Young Justice.*

When did you first start reading comics? I first started reading when I was about twelve, then got back into it at about eighteen.

When was your first professional comics job? My first professional job was assisting for Hoang Nguyen, and my first penciling job was on the *Union* comic for Wildstorm.

What tools of the trade do you use? For penciling, I use a Staedtler or Koh-i-noor lead holder/drafting pencil. For inking, I use a quill with Hunt 101 or 102 nibs. Brushes include Winsor & Newton 2 or 3. For detailing in ink, I often use Micron pens .005 to .03. Nothing bigger than that. Bristol board is best for illustration work. As digital work goes, I have an old 333 MHz Gateway 2000 with about 128 MB of RAM. I use Adobe Photoshop to color illustrations and Adobe Illustrator for more print-ready work.

Who was the biggest professional influence on your work?
My earliest influence was Hoang Nguyen because I was his assistant. At Wildstorm Productions, under Jim Lee, I was forced to really work on my figures and composition. Now, I feel my work is really influenced by Masakazu Katsura. Lastly, I am in awe at the way Carlos Pacheco can compose a page. His camera angles, figure work, and composition are, hands-down, the best.

Your cool artist tip? Develop good work ethics early on. Surround yourself with art and pictures that inspire you. Lastly, don't be afraid to try new things!

CHAPTER 7

Zines: Copy-Shop Comics

Do you think you have to wait until you're older or until you're discovered by a major comic book publisher to make *cool* comics? Think again! You can mass-produce ingenious comics right now that will impress other comics fans and provide exposure for your work.

There are tons of kids across the country who are writing, drawing, and creating their own comic zines—*and* selling them for a profit! Why wait? With a copier, it's easy to put together your own comics for *cheap.*

Zines

Zines are inexpensively produced, self-published, underground publications. The best part about zines is that they can cover just about anything—your zine can include everything from comics, articles, and reviews to poetry and photos. Because zines are so cheap to make, they are a great way to showcase your talents, get feedback on your work from friends, and experiment with new and risky ideas.

It's easy to self-publish your own black-and-white comic zine. Many famous artists got their start in the biz by first publishing their very own comics. Many turned out to be hugely popular. Here are just a few:

Kevin Eastman and Peter Laird's *Teenage Mutant Ninja Turtles*
Dave Sim's *Cerebus*
Brian McDonald and Derek Thompson's *Bindu*
Jeff Smith's *Bone*
Adrian Tomine's *Optic Nerve*
Denis Kitchen's *Mom's Homemade Comics*
Dana Washington's *Blood Shed*

These passionate entrepreneurs all traveled down the self-publishing route. You can, too! Nothing can stop you from publishing your own comic, hot off the presses of your local copy shop!

Making Comics on the Cheap

Though the self-published artists I just mentioned did spend a certain amount of time and money printing their own comics, creating your own comic zine can be way, way cheaper! How much money you want to spend on your creation is up to you—and your budget. If it costs ten cents for each copy of your homemade comic book, you might want to sell them for fifty cents apiece. But if you're just trying to get exposure for your work, you might want to spend as little as possible, with quality still in mind, and give them out for free.

It Came from the Copy Shop!

Making comics at a copy shop is one of the easiest ways to make a quick comic. All you need is your artwork, a few dollars, and the supplies they'll provide you with at the shop: staplers, glue, scissors, and rulers.

How to Make a Copy-Shop Zine

Sizes: Stick with a piece of 8 1/2 x 11 inch paper since it's the size of paper at copy shops. It's easy to bind and you don't have to do any fancy trimming to a smaller size. You can also fold it in half to double the number of pages in your comic.

1. Carefully gather up your completed original artwork for your story. It doesn't matter how many pages—your story could be 8, 16, 22 . . . or 200 pages, if you've *really* been busy! Make sure you have a cover image, too, as well as a title.

2. At the copy shop, make one master copy of your artwork. Use the master to produce the other copies, so you don't have to use your original artwork. Make sure all the pages are in the right order, too. Depending on the size of your original art, you may have to reduce it on the copier to fit. A clerk can help, but if your drawings are on typical art board, you'd have to reduce it by about 60 percent to fit a 8 1/2 x 11 inch sheet of paper.

The people at the copy shop might have some good suggestions and advice, so ask them for help! They can offer assistance and estimate the cost to produce what you have in mind *before* you start making copies.

3. Once you have a master copy, choose your paper and start making copies. Inexpensive, standard white copy paper is great for the interior pages of your comic. Colored paper can be nice for the cover but is not necessary. Just be sure that the colors aren't too dark—you want people to be able to read your homemade comic.

4. When you're done, there are lots of ways to bind your comic together. The easiest and cheapest is to fold it in

Comics Creator—Jon Bogdanove

Jon Bogdanove is the artist on *Superman vs. Aliens 2* and has worked for Marvel Comics on *Power Pack* and *X-Factor*. He started reading comics when he was six years old. Jon began his professional career in comics when he was twenty-seven, working on *Alpha Flight # 32*. His latest work is *The Incredible Hulk*.

What tools of the trade do you use? Mechanical pencils; various pencils with different leads and sizes; two-ply Bristol board, matte finish; two Raphael Kolinsky sable brushes; various pen nibs, but especially Hunts 102 pen nib; and Rapidograph tech pens.

What's your helpful hint on the right way to start a drawing? I like to start with several thumbnail sketches to work out my ideas. Then I may do several construction drawings of the most important images, figures, or gestures. After that, I may do one more thumbnail sketch to reconcile these bits and pieces into a cohesive, fluent page or illustration. I work sloppy, free, and loose. Finally, when it's time to transfer all this work onto the illustration board (using Xerox enlargements and a light box, or artograph projector), I worry about neatness and craft.

Any other advice on breaking into comics you wish someone had told you when you started? Diversify your abilities, education, and experiences as much as possible.

What kinds of drawing utensils do you use or recommend?
I usually just do a fairly loose sketch with color-erase light-blue pencil (NOT repro-blue—too waxy!) and do most of the actual drawing with ink; it's more fun and spontaneous.

I almost never use black-lead pencils. I could never get the hang of brush-inking, so I use a variety of felt-tip markers—Pilot Razor-Points, Berol Boldliners (give a nice brush-like thick and thin line with a bit of pressure, but they do tend to get mushy pretty quickly); Sharpie fine points, Sanford High-Impact, and Prismacolor Dual-Nib markers for large black areas. There are a lot of good White-Out-type correction pens out there, which are much easier to use than the old Liquid Paper brushes. The Bic White-Out pen is decent; my favorite is the Pentel Presto! correction pen. The newer Milky gel roller works pretty well for fine detail fixes. I then use the Staedtler pigment liner permanent ink pen to ink on top of the White-Out. Water-based inks won't dry at all on the correction fluid surface; they'll bead up and smear like crazy.

half. This idea is great for keeping the cost down—though your readers might tend to lose a page here and there. Adding one or two staples should help keep your comic book in one piece. And there you have it—a bound comic to sell or give to family and friends!

Homemade Comics . . . Just Like Mom Used to Make?

Okay, so your mom doesn't make homemade comic books, but there are some ways *you* can give your comics that personal, homemade touch. Aside from autographing your comics, which is a unique thing to do, there are many ways to make a rare, specially-created comic book just for your readers. You may have loads of ideas yourself, but in case you don't, here are just a few to get you started.

Interactive comics: Create a mystery comic that the reader has to solve by posing a question at the end of each page, such as, "If you think the robot butler filled the bathtub with chocolate sauce, turn to page 9. If you think the circus clown did it, turn to page 12." Let the reader determine the direction of the story. The story will be different for each person reading it.

Sketchbook comics: You can use sketches from your idea journal for your comic book. Make copies of the best pages and bind them into a limited-edition book. Every month or so, do a new volume of your "Don't Believe the Hype Sketchbook 2001" or "My Best Work, So Far: Summer Edition." Make sets for yourself that chronicle your best comics and sketches from the year. You can also give them to friends, editors, family members, and art teachers, so they can see how you've improved.

Mixed-media comics: Cut pictures and phrases out of magazines and newspapers, glue in pieces of fabric, or color pages by hand to make the comics pop right off the page. This way, each reader gets a comic you made by hand, just for them. If you know the person well, you can personalize the comic with things you know they'll like.

Super-coolest mini-comic ever! Andi Watson is the creator of comics like *Skeleton Key, Breakfast After Noon,* and *Slow News Day* . He's also popularized a great format for a cool mini-comic. Follow the instructions and diagram below to make your *own* mini-comic!

1. Choose a piece of white paper and trim the paper to 8 1/4 inches wide x 5 3/4 inches high.

2. Fold the paper in half, lengthwise. Next, fold it in half again, but this time widthwise. Then fold it one more time, widthwise.

3. Now unfold the paper and lay it flat. You should have eight rectangles marked by the folds (see Example A). Each rectangle will represent one of your panels. With your scissors, cut a slit in the center margin that separates the four panels in the center of the page (follow the dotted lines in Example A for your cut). Cut *only* this section.

4. Use each panel in your mini-comic to illustrate your story. *Only* illustrate one side of the paper. Note: Make sure that the tops of your characters' bodies are at the top of each panel; the tops point toward the center margin (see Example B).

Example A	Example B
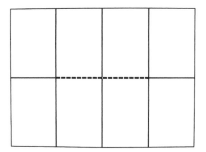	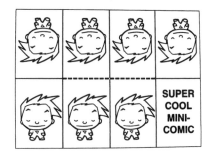

5. When your illustrations are complete, fold the paper again, lengthwise (see Example C). Your art should be facing out with the blank side of the paper facing in. With your fingers on the four center panels—two on each side of the fold—create an *x* shape with the paper as if you're looking at it from above (see Example D). Then fold it so that the shape resembles an open book.

Example C

Example D

SUPER COOL MINI-COMIC

Example E

6. Now press the paper flat, like you're closing a book (see Example E). You should have a mini-comic book! If you unfold the paper and lay it flat again, you can bring it to the copy shop, where you can copy as many comics as you want on different colors of paper. When you get home, trim and fold the copies up in the exact same way to make tons more mini-comics. Put your name and contact info on the back cover so people can get in touch with you if they want more comics.

That's it! Six easy steps to creating your own mini-comic that you can give as gifts, trade, mail, and use to promote and display your work. Before you know it, you'll have people waiting in line for the next story!

Collaborative comics: Invite a group of friends over for a comic book brainstorming session. Maybe one of you has a fantastic character idea but doesn't know how to fit it into a story. Perhaps you have been working out a story line for the past few weeks but just can't seem to draw the right character. It can be a real blast producing comics with a group of friends who share your creative spirit.

Postcard comics: One of my favorite ideas is making postcards into comic strips! Find out from the post office how much a standard postcard costs and what the maximum size can be. You should be able to fit two postcards on one piece of 8 1/2 inch x 11 inch paper, with trimming (be sure to get heavier paper, like cardstock).

The first postcard is the first panel of art, and the second postcard picks up the story from the first. Make ten copies of your art at the copy shop, and ask a clerk to trim them to individual postcard size. You'll be left with ten copies of each postcard. Send out the first one to friends, neighbors, other artists, editors, and publishers the first week. The next week, send out the second. Keep doing this as long as you like. You may have a suspense-filled story that runs for weeks or even months . . . all on a series of handy postcards!

Celebrate!

This is the best part of the comic bookmaking process, because you finally get to see all your hard work in a final product. It doesn't matter how you make your first comic, whether it's a copy-shop comic, a zine, a mini-comic, or something else. Whatever it is, be extra *proud* of your creation. Celebrate! Treat yourself to an ice cream sundae or banana split. Splurge on a double cheeseburger, nachos piled with all the fixin's, or pizza with all the toppings. Then sit back and read your very first comic book. You're officially a comics creator!

YOUNG ARTIST PROFILE

Sabrina-Marie Bell, age 16

Sabrina-Marie Bell loves to draw. She's a big fan of manga and anime, and will read and watch as much of it as she can. She brings that influence to her art.

When did you first start reading comics?
Three or four years ago, at my friend's house.

What's your favorite comic book?
My favorite comic is *Sailor Moon*.

Who has had the biggest influence on your work?
Japanese comic artist, Naoko Takeuchi. I aspire to be like the great Naoko and make a great comic known throughout the world.

Why do you like to draw?
Since I'm interested in anime, I've always enjoyed making my own artwork of my favorite anime characters.

How often do you draw?
Every day, all day long, and every other chance I get!

What's your own supercool idea for a comic book character?
A medieval, magical goddess and her trials through evil forces.

What cool things have you done to get your comics noticed?
I dressed in my own costume to be my comic character.

What inspires you most?
Everything anime and manga!

CHAPTER 8

Self-Promotion: Getting Publicity for Your Work

In your backpack, you have your copy-shop zine, your mini-comic, or your groundbreaking graphic novel! But what do you *do* with it? How do you get the word out to all your future fans?

Big comic book companies spend loads of money to get the word out about their newest projects, but there are several easy and inexpensive ways to get exposure for your comics without investing a lot of time or money. Here are clever strategies that you can employ to market and distribute your comic.

Art contests: One great way to get exposure for your comics is to enter art contests as often as you can. It's good practice, and you can win some sweet prizes! Comics magazines like *Wizard* run comic contests frequently. Your local newspaper may also feature kids' art in its comics section. Check out the resource section of this book for more contest information!

Colleen Doran, sole creator of *A Distant Soil* and Aria Press, was scouted by a comic book publisher at a convention when she was just 15 years old!

Bookstore bound: There are many independent bookstores devoted entirely to small-press comics, indie comics, and zines. If there's a bookstore like this in your town, ask the owner or manager if he or she is willing to carry your comic zine. Even if the owner can't sell them, they might have a freebie table, where you can leave a stack for anyone who wants one.

Giveaways: You can also make giveaways based on your comic book characters. For my comic, *Sky Ape,* we made a one-of-a-kind handmade *Sky Ape* stuffed animal and raffled it off to one lucky reader! We also relabeled Hershey's chocolate nuggets with *Sky Ape* comic art and called them "monkey nuggets."

Hangin' around: If your local comic store or coffee shop does art exhibitions, ask if you could display some of your original artwork in the store. Schools are also a fantastic place to display your work. Perhaps your art teacher can help coordinate a comic book art show or hallway exhibit.

Garage sale comics: Try making up a bunch of comics and selling them when your family has a yard sale. Charge a nickel to a quarter for a mini-comic, and sign it for the reader. People will get a collector's item that few others have!

A little something extra: Do you know someone who owns a local pizza place, bakery, or take-out restaurant? Make up a stack of mini-comics and ask if they'd mind putting one in the box or bag for anyone who orders take-out. Every month, do a new mini-comic that continues the story from the first one, and so on. You'll have a whole bunch of hooked fans just waiting for the next exciting issue!

There are thousands of ways to promote your work. Always keep a few

Do you know what a Hawaiian beverage company used to do? Under the caps of their bottled fruit juices, they included a little cardboard disc with different kinds of art on it. Eventually, these became collector's items known as POGs. "POG" stands for "Pineapple Orange Guava," a kind of juice.

Comics Creator—Chynna Clugston-Major

Chynna Clugston-Major began her self-declared addiction to comics by reading *Archie* when she was five years old. She began her own comics career at age twenty-one, when she drew stories for *Dark Horse Presents*. Chynna is currently the creator of her own comic, *Blue Monday*, in addition to working as a flashback artist on *Hopeless Savages*.

When did you first start reading comics? As far as comics go, I read only things like *Archie* and *Mad Magazine* until I was about eleven, around the time *The Watchmen* came out. I had been surrounded by mainstream comics growing up, but they weren't mine, and they bored me, to be honest. I needed laughs. . .but *The Watchmen* blew me away. After that, I thought I'd look around a bit . . . discovered *Love and Rockets*, *Dirty Pair*, *Pirate Corps*, and *Deadline Magazine* with *Tank Girl* and *Wired World*. It was all over for me—I got totally addicted.

Who is the biggest professional influence on your work? That's difficult to say . . . it'd probably have to be Rumiko Takahashi. Being the most successful female comic creator ever (to me anyway) with an astounding amount of readers worldwide, she's a major source of inspiration and helped me grow to love Japanese comic books. *Lum* was my first real exposure to manga. I'm even more fond of *Maison Ikkoku* . . . Takahashi just has the greatest sense of humor.

Any advice for a budding comics artist, especially a girl?
The best thing I can say is, try to ignore the people who treat you differently because you're female. The ones who say, "You draw pretty good . . .for a girl" or "I hate chick creators . . ." They don't realize how dumb they are being and should be pitied for their stupidity! Also, don't try to just create things you think the public would enjoy. Do what makes you happy, what's special or relevant to what you care about or stand for, and you'll be all the better for it.

mini-comics with you.
If you go to a local
comic book conven-
tion, pass them out to
potential fans. You can easily
use mini-comics as business cards
by including your contact information on the back cover. Before you
know it, you'll have your very own
die-hard fans, and your work will have a
good chance of getting into the hands of editors and publishers who could eventually hire you to work on a big-
time comic!

Sergio Aragonés, creator of *Groo*, emigrated to America in 1962. His cartoon was turned down by several smaller publications and finally picked up by *MAD* magazine. Sergio has been working for *MAD* ever since.

Promote Yourself!

Promoting your comics can be as much fun as making the comic itself. Chances are, you'll have ideas to publicize your work that no one has ever even thought of. Remember these hints: Be as creative as possible; use the resources right around you; and try not to spend a lot of money, if you can help it. Personalize comics with your signature. Draw original sketches on envelopes or small paper bags and put the comic inside as a gift. The sky is the limit on what you can do with simple materials, pas-sion, and imagination.

YOUNG ARTIST PROFILE

Kristoffer Smith, age 16

Kris borrowed money from his parents to set up a table at a comic convention in Pittsburgh. Then, he paid them back by doing caricatures of people at the show. It also helped him promote his own comic book.

When did you first start reading comics? I read my first comic book in the fourth grade, Joe Madureira's work on *The X Men*.

What's your favorite comic book? While I'm a fan of *SpyBoy* and I enjoyed the *Battle Gods* series, my favorite comic book is *Battlechasers*, naturally.

What sort of tools do you use while drawing? A blue pencil, a mechanical pencil, a .005 pen for thin lines, 1.0 for medium lines, Sharpies for character outlines and boxes, and jumbo permanent markers for fill-ins.

What comic book artists have had the most influence on your work? Joe Madureira, Louis Small, Jr. *(Vampirella, Ka-zar)*—who is a good friend of mine—and my art teacher Kyra Schon.

Why do you want to be a comic book artist? Comics are the best. I've been into them for sooo long, and I've been drawing since before I can remember. I have Mighty Mouse pictures I drew before I was in school.

Why do you like to draw? I don't know ... it's like a passion. I think it's my influences. With all the inspiration, I just have to keep drawing and keep getting better.

What's your favorite stuff to draw? Manga, my comic book, and watercolor self-portraits.

How often do you draw? At least an hour every day—honestly!

Do you take art classes now? I go to C.A.P.A. (Creative and Performing Arts) high school. It's a high school where kids can specialize in certain forms of the arts like dancing, singing—or like me—visual arts.

Do you plan on going to art school? I would most like to attend S.V.A.—it's the New York School for Visual Arts—and afterwards, maybe an internship, or work for a major publisher like Dark Horse.

What are you currently working on? My idea for a character is my own signature character, Sirk. He is a guy who has the powers of the krossej; anyways, it's a really cool character. You all can catch the fun in my upcoming book, *Sirk*. Stay tuned to www.vortexkomix.net for updates.

What cool things have you done to break into comics? I try to meet as many important people as I can; keep my own small-press comic going; and practice, practice, practice!

What inspires you? Everything—school, movies, music. I learned a lot about perspective from geometry. My friends are big inspirations also, because we all have our special unique feature, and we can learn from each other.

CHAPTER 9

Portfolios: Submitting Your Comics to Publishers

You've been working hard making your own comics, filling your sketchbook with great ideas, and creating comics with friends. But, what's next? How do you get from there to working on your favorite comic for a big publisher?

When I was a kid, my cousin Joe sent for art submissions guidelines from Marvel Comics. He spent every weekend drawing furiously and eventually sent hundreds of art samples to the editors. Sometimes, he'd hear back from an editor, and even if it was critical feedback (Joe was a talented artist and eventually got accepted to Rhode Island School of Design), he would explode with joy! The fact that someone was *reviewing* his work was all he needed. It helped spur him to keep drawing.

Portfolio Review

If you're at that point where a critique of your work will assist in moving you to the next level as an artist, you may want to save up some money to attend a comic book convention. Hopefully, there will be one relatively close to you. Check the web sites in the resource section of this book for more info.

The San Diego Comic-Con, my personal favorite, is usually held in July or August. For the past eight years, I've been attending the convention, and every year, I do portfolio reviews with new artists. Most conventions have these reviews, but ask before you plan your trip.

Each editor or reviewer looks for different styles and ideas. Below is some advice on how to present yourself and your work, what editors will want to see from you, and what you can expect from the portfolio review experience.

Be professional: Your review starts before the editor looks at your portfolio. When you're standing in line, don't brag about how good you are. Don't insult anyone else's work. An editor should *never* judge you on what you wear, what kind of comics you like, or where you're from, but you don't want to sling a bad attitude their way.

Most importantly, be yourself and relax. You have a lot to feel confident about!

Bill Waterson had great difficulty in finding a taker for his comic *Calvin and Hobbes* until Universal Press Syndicate accepted it in 1985 with absolutely no expectations of the huge success it would have.

Be organized: Know exactly what you want to show an editor, and organize your presentation beforehand. Don't shuffle through pages during your review, and be prepared to answer any questions the editor might have about your work.

Show your comics: Most editors want to see sequential art and aren't as interested in cover art, single illustrations, paintings, or sketches. They want to see if you can tell a story on a comics page. If an editor *asks* to see that other work, *then* you can show it. Also, show only your best comics work, not all of your work.

Listen: You may have to wait in line for a while before your work is reviewed, so once you're up at bat, make the most of it. Listen to what the editors have to say. You don't have to follow all of their advice, but at least hear them out. They're there to help you, and chances are, they'll give you wonderful direction.

What to expect: Don't assume you'll be hired on *Gen13* after one review. You're really there for feedback. But you have every right to expect a focused, professional editor who will give you specific guidance to improve your comics. Take in all the sights of the show, meet with other creators like yourself, and see your favorite artists in person. It can be a great experience to be surrounded by hundreds of other people who enjoy comics as much as you do!

Have fun: Of course, have fun! This isn't boot camp. Enjoy yourself, and revel in the experience of sharing your work with comics professionals.

Submissions Guidelines

If you can't make it to a comics convention, you can always submit your work through the mail. It's important to know that each company has very specific submission guidelines. Most companies post that information on their web sites, and you can also call and ask them to mail submissions information (see resource list at back). If they don't accept submissions, nothing's stopping you from sending them periodic copies of your mini-comic or postcard comic as a gift. They might like what they see, and then—BAM!—you're on your way!

    If you're aiming to be hired or commissioned by a company, it takes time. Chynna Clugston-Major showed Oni Press editor Jamie Rich her comics portfolio for four

Comics Creator—Mark Schultz

Mark is the award-winning creator, writer, and artist of *Xenozoic Tales*; the co-creator of *SubHuman*; a cover artist contributor for *Star Wars*; and is also the writer of *Superman: The Man of Steel, Aliens vs. Predator vs. Terminator, Predator: Hell and Hot Water, Aliens Apocalypse,* and *Aliens: Havoc.*

When did you first start reading comics? I was six, in the first grade, when I first saw (or, at least, recognized) comics. Fellow classmates would bring them to school—the one that made a lasting impression was the first appearance of the *Metal Men* in Showcase.

What's your favorite comic book? Of all time? Impossible to say—if you discount my self-serving devotion to *Xenozoic Tales.* EC's science fiction and war books would have to be up there near the top, as would Eisner's *Spirit* sections, Lee and Kirby's run on the *Fantastic Four,* and Joe Kubert's *Hawkman.*

Did you go to art school, or are you self-taught? I graduated from Kutztown State University with a B.F.A. in painting. I think it was very important that I received a rounded education in art and the humanities, even though at the time I attended (the mid-70s), art schools were not particularly receptive to the idea of comics as a respectable medium of expression. But college taught me how to learn for myself (the most important lesson) and introduced me to lots of avenues, directions, and disciplines that have helped me immensely to develop as both an artist and a writer.

Your cool artist tip for a newcomer comics artist? Be diverse! Don't settle for just being a penciler, an inker, or a writer. Learn every aspect of the craft of creating and producing a comic, from generating original ideas to understanding the printing process. Assume control of your career.

What's your best hint for the right way to start an illustration or sequential comics page/strip? Be patient about developing your idea. Do small, fast comps on scrap paper to just play around with different variations on your idea before you ever commit to the board you'll do the actual finished art on. You'll catch and solve problems much easier in the scrap-paper stage than in the finished stage—and you may be surprised how your original thoughts grow and evolve for the better when you are not under the pressure of doing it "right" the first time.

103

consecutive years before she was hired! But, in all that time, she never stopped perfecting her art and working on her *own* comics. Eventually, they published her comic, *Blue Monday*, and it's one of the coolest comics around!

The Comics Biz

Just as each company has different guidelines on what they look for in a new artist or project, each also has different terms on which they'll hire you or publish your work. Many companies use terms you might not have heard before, so here's a crash course on some basics that will help.

Contract: A contract is a legal document that you and the publisher sign, showing that you've both come to an agreement on what you'll produce and what he'll publish. There's a lot of information in a contract, so when you get to this stage, you'll definitely want a lawyer to look at it with you.

Work for hire: Most popular comics, such as *Spider-Man, The Hulk,* and *Green Lantern* are done as "work for hire." That means you are being hired to draw for an existing comic that the company owns or is licensing (for example, Dark Horse licenses *Star Wars* from Lucasfilm). You will be paid for your work, but you won't own what you create. However, you should have every right to keep your original art. Make sure that's part of the deal!

Creator-owned: If something is creator-owned, it means that you retain the copyright. That's just a fancy way of saying no one can do anything with your comic unless you legally let them, whether you publish it yourself or have someone else do it. For example, Chynna Clugston-Major owns *Blue Monday*, but it's published by Oni Press; my friends and I own *Sky Ape*, but it's published by PlanetLar.

Vouchers: At most companies, you voucher for your work once it's completed. If you've finished drawing an issue of *Buffy the Vampire Slayer*, you'd send a voucher (a slip of paper with payment info) to your editor, letting him know how many pages you did and what to pay you.

Page rate: When you work on a comic like *X-Men* or *WildC.A.T.S.*, you get money for every page you do. This is determined before you start working, and it's stated in your contract. Page rates vary widely, depending on the book. You might get

The first three anthologies of *The Far Side*, by Gary Larson, were on the *NY Times* bestseller list and sold over six million copies by 1987.

$150 to $200 just to pencil a comics page of *Superman*. You might get more. On creator-owned projects, you might get less but you keep ownership of what you create.

Royalty: Sound scary? It isn't. It just means that in addition to getting a page rate, you might get some money later if the book you work on sells really well. If a book makes $100 profit, you might get $1, $10, or more, depending on the percentage in your contract.

It's good to *really* learn the ins and outs of contracts at some point. Don't be intimidated by them. It's important stuff to learn, but it's still fun. It's part of the process once you become the artist on *Witchblade, Planet of the Apes, Green Arrow,* or your other favorites, or on your very own creation. Contracts are part of the business once you're a pro!

Garfield by Jim Davis, is translated into seven languages and published in 22 countries. The character appears on more than 3,000 products and is marketed in 28 countries.

The Big Time!

Now you've hit the big time. Your comics art is ready to be reviewed by editors and publishers of big comics companies. Maybe you'll be the next artist on *Spider-Man* or *Star Wars*. Maybe you'll get to create your very own comic, with characters you designed and stories you wrote. You've already proven that you can make great comics on your own, so be confident when you show your work to others, whether it be an art teacher at school or a comics editor at a portfolio review. They might have feedback on how to make your work better. A publisher might not have work for you right away. That's okay, and not something to discourage you. Remember, it's your love of comics that got you this far. Whatever might happen, you're *already* a success!

YOUNG ARTIST PROFILE

Josh Covey, age 17

Josh Covey has been drawing comics for thirteen years. His favorite original character is a strong-willed woman, Valla, who fights battles to the death in a coliseum. He also enjoys drawing Laura Croft and hopes to one day work on *Tomb Raider* comics.

What sort of experience have you tried to get in the comic book industry?
I have had a few jobs here and there that have helped me. I've worked on a video game, doing all the character designs. I have had experience working on comics and had a job working on a book cover and some inside art. Though it never got published, I learned a lot from working on this book. Page layouts got easier and easier.

Have you ever tried to enter a contest?
I have only entered around five contests in my whole life, of which I have won one.

Who is your favorite character to draw?
Lara Croft is one of my favorite characters of all time. I never really liked drawing other people's characters, but she's just so easy to draw. You could do any kind of scene you wanted with her, and it would still look great. I love the video game *Tomb Raider* and always thought just how cool it would be if they would make a comic of it. When I found out that they were, I thought, "Man, it can't get any better than this!" Two of my favorite things all in one—how could you beat that! So, if I do get into comics, that's the one I want to work in. Though, if I don't get to work on *Tomb Raider* I'm not going to give up.

Do you feel like you're ready to submit your comics to a publisher?
I have never tried to submit anything to comic book companies. I've finally gotten where I want to be with my art. I guess that's why I never wanted to submit anything—I was never really quite ready for it. But I am now—100 percent. Drawing comics is what I have always wanted to do; it's been a life-long dream that I hope someday comes true.

What things do you use to create your comics?
For penciling, I use a Staedtler MARS-780 Architects pencil. For erasers, I

use the Pentel clic erasers and the Sanford Tuff Stuff stick erasers. And for inking, I use just a fine ballpoint Bic ink pen. And paper, just about anything that doesn't have a slick surface.

What's your advice to other kid comics artists?

Most of all, spend as much time as you can with your art. Be patient—this is not something you can just rush into and be a pro at. And find a large variety of artists to study. It will help you out more than you know. It'll allow you to do all kinds of things with your art—you won't be limited. I followed artists like Jim Lee and Mike Mignola, Sam Keith to Adam Hughes. So, my art is just a mixture of all kinds, and I'm still trying to find that spot where everything fits just perfectly. I've been going at this for more than thirteen years, and I still have a ways to go, but it'll be worth the wait.

Where do you get your ideas?

Most of my ideas just come straight to me when I sit down to draw. But when I have what I guess you would call an artist's block, I just turn on TV shows like *Farscape* or cartoons like *Gundam*. Other than that, I just read books and find anything that has to do with art.

Who is your favorite character that you've created?

Valla. She is, in a way, a gladiator. Only, take away everything but the coliseum and put in giant mechs, like the ones you would see in *Gundam*. The world that she lives in is harsh, much like the Dark Ages.

CHAPTER 10

Beyond Comic Books: Hollywood Directing to Video Game Designing

Ever wonder what's beyond comics? Comic books are the center of the creative universe for a legion of talented directors, artists, musicians, writers, producers, video game designers, and animators. They've learned what you already know: that there's something magical in comics that crosses all boundaries and is governed only by your imagination. But how do you get from comics to all those other careers? Let's find out!

The Comic Book Clique

Many comic book companies divide the work for creating a comic book into more specialized positions. There are lots of production people behind the scenes that you never hear about. The artists and creators are often part of an assembly line of talented people. Here are a few more specialized jobs in comics.

Creator: A comic book creator comes up with the idea or concept behind the comic book. They may or may not do all the art or writing, but they are the ones with the creative vision behind the comic.

Writer: The writer comes up with the story and the script for the comic. He or she will break the story down by panel and also write instructions and scene descriptions for the penciler.

Penciler: The penciler draws the comic, but only in pencil. He or she begins by sketching thumbnails that follow the comic script, leaving extra room in each panel for the text. Then, the penciler draws the final penciled illustrations on Bristol board.

Inker: The inker uses brushes, crow quills, or Pigma pens to go over the penciler's pages in black ink. This makes the page easier to reproduce into a finished comic.

Letterer: Letterers draw the word balloons, captions, and the text. This is usually done between the pencil and ink stage. They use rulers to measure the letters so that they are all the same height. Lettering can also be done with computers, using desktop programs like Adobe Pagemaker and QuarkXpress.

Colorist: After the comic is inked, the art is scanned and color is added using computer software programs like Adobe Photoshop. Some colorists still use paints to color the comics, but this is becoming less common.

Editor: The editor guides the entire process of creating the comic, from the creator's inception to proofreading the writer's words, as well as working closely with the pencilers, inkers, letterers, and colorists.

Cool Comics-Related Jobs

If you like comics, you don't have to limit yourself to jobs in the comic book industry. Comics can give you a foundation for other forms of creativity. The options are limitless! You could design video games, write for TV, work on a movie, direct a music video, or produce an animated series. Here are just a few of the comics-related jobs out there.

Video game developer: Imagine designing the latest game for Nintendo or Playstation. That's what video

Comics Creator—Bruce Timm

**Bruce Timm is a producer for *Batman: the Animated Series,
Superman, Batman Beyond,* and, most currently, *Justice League.***

When did you become interested in comics? I started reading comics
seriously in 1973—when I was twelve.

Do you have a favorite comic? It's hard for me to pick just one; there are
so many! I guess I'd have to say anything by Jack Kirby— *The Fantastic
Four*, probably. My favorite current comic is Mike Mignola's *Hellboy*.

How did you start drawing comics for a living? I began my "pro" comics
work when I was twenty-three, with Mattel's *He-Man Masters of the
Universe* line of action figures. I drew the mini-comics that were packaged
with the toys.

Have you ever taken classes on how to draw comics? Outside of a few
life-drawing classes, I'm almost completely self-taught.

**What feedback would you give to young, aspiring comic book
artists?** Be open to criticism. Do your best work,
show it to editors and art direc-
tors, and if they reject you,
don't take it personally.
Listen to their criticism. Try
to apply it to your next batch
of samples, and resubmit it. I
have gotten a ton of rejec-
tions—sometimes from artists
whose work I personally didn't
like or respect. And boy, did I
hate being told my work wasn't
good enough! But in hindsight, I'd
have to say that most of their
points were absolutely valid, and
their criticisms and suggestions
dead-on. So, keep an open mind;
toughen up; and keep drawing, drawing, all the time, drawing!

The Mask ™ © Dark Horse Comics, Inc.
All rights reserved.

game developers do; they work as programmers, animators, art directors, and video game testers—people whose job it is to test for glitches in game play! Your ability to draw comics can translate into 3-D designs for computer games. Eric Kohler, for example, designs comic book covers and also creates video game characters for Monolith PC games.

Production artist: Visualize being behind the scenes of your favorite movie or designing some of the characters in the movie. You can use what you've learned as a comic book artist and apply it to one of the most creative jobs in movies, production artist. Brian O'Connell and Derek Thompson are two artist friends who both really enjoy comics. Their dream came true when they got to work on some big-time comic books, like *Aliens vs. Predator*. Then they used their comic book knowledge and experience to become production artists, working on character designs for *Star Wars* and other top-secret movie projects!

Scriptwriter: Scriptwriters work in a variety of media. You can write screenplays for movies, as well as teleplays for TV shows and animated series. You can even create the story for video games. Screenplays and teleplays are very similar to comics scripts, so if you're writing for your own comic, you *already* have a good idea of how to write scripts in general. Evan Dorkin is known in comics for his hilarious *Milk and Cheese, Dork, Hectic Planet*, and others. He took the mechanics of writing comics scripts and adapted his skills to write for the animated TV show, *Space Ghost Coast to Coast*.

The names of the Pokemon characters are changed based upon the country that the TV show or movie is being shown in, forcing the Pokemon creators to come up with over 500 names. Pikachu is the only character whose name is the same across all countries.

Producer: The title of producer can mean different things. On a movie it's generally the person managing the finances. On video games, and animated TV shows, it's the person with the unifying vision behind the project—more like a film director. The producer conceives the story, designs the characters and settings, directs the storyboard artists, animators, and voice actors. Scott Morse, creator of the comic book *Ancient Joe*, is also a producer for Cartoon Network's *Ferret and Parrot*. He used the skills he honed as a comic book artist to create the characters for his cartoon.

Cartoon creator: A cartoon creator comes up with an idea for a cartoon and then helps produce, design, or draw it. Comic book artists Bruce Timm and Scott Marse created their own comics and then transformed their ideas into cartoon versions. Comics artist Matt Groening, author of the comic *Life in Hell*, came up with the immensely popular animated series, *The Simpsons* and *Futurama*. He's come a long way from doodles of rabbits named Binky and Bongo.

Did you know that the film director of Clerks, Kevin Smith, likes comics so much that he's written for Daredevil and Green Arrow, created his own Clerks comic, and owns his own comic book store?

Storyboard artists:
Storyboard artists are an unseen part of the film-making process, but a very important one. These artists are the ones working with the director to pace out the entire film, TV show, or animated series in scene-by-scene drawings. Storyboards show setting; the placement of characters in frame; and the main conflicts, action, or resolves. Chances are, whatever your favorite movie or cartoon is, there's a talented storyboard artist behind it.

Film director: A director is the person with the unifying vision behind a film. The actors, production designers, costume designers, editors, and pretty much anyone else involved with the creative aspects of the movie take their cues from the director. The result is the seamless vision you see on the screen. British artist Jamie Hewlett is the creator of the riotous comic, *Tank Girl*. He's seen his character made into a blockbuster movie and now gets to direct music videos for the British band, Gorillaz, featuring members of Blur, with the cartoon characters he created.

Comics publisher: A comics publisher, like Mike Richardson of Dark Horse comics or Jim Lee of Wildstorm, is the person commissioning the line of cool comics you see on the shelf of your favorite comics store. If DC Comics is publishing a new *Doom Patrol* series or Marvel is revamping *The X-Men*, the publisher is involved, on some significant level, with the decision. Jim Lee started as an artist on comics like *The X-Men*. Eventually, he went on to become the publisher of Wildstorm, whose books include *Wild-C.A.T.S., Mr. Majestic, The Authority,* and *Gen13*.

Toy creator: Todd McFarlane is the creator of the popular comic *Spawn*, which was made into a hit movie. Aside from publishing comics, his company also produces some of the best monster-creature action figures ever made. He got his start working on comics like *GI Joe, Batman,* and *Spider-Man*. Eventually he created an empire of hyper-detailed and diverse lines of toy figures, including Austin Powers, The Beatles: Yellow Submarine, Spawn, and Creech.

> Dale Keown, who helped create the "new" Hulk in 1990, taught himself how to draw while on the road between concerts with his band.

There's no one, simple way to get a job as a storyboard artist for a big movie or as a character designer for a video game company. The best thing to do, when you're ready, is to write those companies letters and include samples of your art. Tell them what position you're interested in and why you think you'd be a good candidate. If there isn't a position open at the time, ask them to give you some feedback on breaking into those other careers. Who knows, maybe Nintendo or Miramax will soon be calling you!

Your Life as a Comic Book Artist

So, you wanna be a comic book artist? SHZZAM! You already are! If you want to draw comics simply for your own pleasure, that's great. If you want to go on to become a professional and get paid to do something you love, that's great too. Its all up to you. In this book, you've discovered some tips on how to start a studio, write stellar stories, create fascinating characters, draw great strips, and show your work to the world. Now you can use these hints to create the best comic book of your life. Remember, you're never too young to do something you love. So start drawing now!

YOUNG ARTIST PROFILE

Becky Cloonan, age 20

Becky Cloonan lives in New York City, where she draws her comics from her apartment in Queens. She is in her third year of animation at the School of Visual Arts. After graduation, she plans to continue a career in art.

When did you first start reading comics? My dad used to read me *Silver Surfer* for bedtime stories when I was in elementary school. I was basically a Marvel girl until middle school, when I got into Japanese-style comics and was taken by the different styles and genres available there.

What's your favorite comic book of all time? That's tricky . . . I guess either *Kabuki, Blade of the Immortal, Sin City,* or *Transmetropolitan.*

What are your favorite tools to draw with? A Bic mechanical pencil (.7 or .5), Rapidographs (.8 and .35), quill, sumi brush, fingers . . . anything within reach. Oh, and lots of erasers.

What person has had the greatest effect on your work? I've had so many influences in the past, I can't name one specific person, but watching a lot of films had a large impact on the way I compose my comics. Other people who've influenced my art are David Mack, Yoshitaka Amano, Teddy Kristiansen, Keiko Nishi, and Matthew Woodson.

Why do you want to be a comic book artist? I'm really attracted to story-telling, plus it's a very visual medium (and since I love to write and draw, that's perfect). Although I'm interested in so many other things as well—film, animation, photography, painting, fashion—I'd like to try everything I can. But in comics, I can combine my art with my writing, fashion, photography, and cinematography; and that can be very gratifying.

What's your favorite subject to draw? Cute punker boys [laughs]. My favorite stuff is drawing slice-of-life short stories, as well as period pieces—big dresses and strange costumes. I try to capture a mood rather than a pretty picture.

How often do you draw? I draw all the time—about four to five hours a day.

What comics are you currently working on? I have an on-line strip about Johnny, a recovering punk rocker, and his jaded adventures (something along those lines, it's pretty silly as well as socially conscious).

Another comic I'm working on is Johnny ten years earlier, which I plan on self-publishing. Yet another is a play I wrote in revenge-tragedy style, drawn like a comic. I have so many ideas, I realized the only way I'll finish them all is to make them really short; most of my comics now are between eight and fifteen pages.

What cool things have you already done to break into comics? I am in a studio with four other girls, and we've self-published two books. Other than that, I just do freelance gigs and go to conventions to show my artwork around (when I'm not distracted by all the comics).

What inspires you most? A lot of my inspiration comes from music (punk and indie rock) and old Expressionist films. I'm moved by life in general, and a lot of things that happen around me I put into my comics, making them realistic to a point, but then kind of surreal. Also, seeing other peoples' artwork helps. I live with other artists, and my friends are always drawing. That in itself is enough to make me continue.

Resources: Recommended Industry Info

To be a successful comics artist, it's a good idea to immerse yourself in the world of comics. Below is a helpful mish-mash of comics, instructional books, web sites, and more on this amazing art form.

Drawing Instruction

The Art of Comic Book Inking. Gary Martin and Steve Rude. Portland, Oregon; Dark Horse Comics, 1997. This might just be the *only* comprehensive guide to comic book inking. Not merely instruction for pen-and-ink technique, comics professionals show you the tips and tricks of the trade for the highly specialized field of inking comics.

Comics & Sequential Art. Will Eisner. Tamarac, Florida; Poorhouse Press, 1985. Considered by many to be the first and last word on the mechanics and language of comics, Eisner offers thought-provoking theory and analysis on what makes comics, well . . . comics. It's required reading for anyone serious about the art form.

The Complete Cartooning Course: Principles, Practices, Techniques. Steve Edgell, Brad Brooks, and Tim Pilcher. Hauppauge, New York; Barron's, 2001. This is possibly one of the coolest guides on making comics. It's filled with pages of photos of sample artist studios and materials, *and* art that stretches the complete stylistic horizon.

Draw the Marvel Comics Super Heroes. John Romita, various. Palo Alto, California; Klutz, 1995. The nice thing about this book is that it comes with pens, so you draw right in the book as you learn each lesson. It's great fun and a refreshing change from stuffy instruction books.

Dynamic Figure Drawing. Burne Hogarth. New York, New York; Watson-Guptill, 1979. Hogarth's famous books have been essential instruction for generations of artists. There are several books in the series. *Dynamic Figure Drawing* offers insight into anatomy and pose, while *Dynamic Light and Shadow* gives helpful clues for graduating into mastery of shading and contrast.

How to Draw Cartoon Animation. Preston Blair. Laguna Hills, California; Walter Foster, 1980. The late animator, Preston Blair, worked on some of the biggest cartoons for Disney, MGM, and Hanna-Barbera. This book is packed with priceless, step-by-step instructions to help you perfect facial expressions, body structure, and body movement. Every page showcases Blair's amazing art.

How to Draw Comics the Marvel Way. Stan Lee and John Buscema. New York; New York. Simon & Schuster, 1978. Though first published in the 70s, this is still one of the classic comics guides. Believe it or not, it's all here: perspective, composition, storytelling, expression, technique. . .and who better than Stan, "the Man," and legend John Buscema to show you!

Perspective for Comic Book Artists. David Chelsea. New York, New York; Watson Guptill, 1997. David Chelsea offers the only painstakingly intense guide specifically for comics artists to understand and execute correct perspective. What makes it so great is that he does it *with* comics!

Superheroes: Joe Kubert's Wonderful World of Comics. Joe Kubert. New York, New York; Watson-Guptill, 1999. Joe Kubert is one of the more inspiring creators of classic adventure comics. He's also the founder of the Kubert School, a college dedicated specifically to comics illustration. This book distills Joe's wisdom into a guide that's both accessible to beginners *and* helpful to professionals honing their craft.

Understanding Comics. Scott McCloud. New York; HarperPerennial, 1993. Not since Eisner's *Comics and Sequential Art* has a book come along to deconstruct the mechanics of comics in such an exhaustive manner. McCloud uses comics to teach its history and language, and offers exciting thoughts on the nature of the medium and the base elements of successful storytelling.

Comics History

The Art of Jack Kirby. Ray Wyman, Jr. Orange, California; The Blue Rose Press, 1992. Captain America. The Hulk. The New Gods. You know the names in his pantheon of superheroes, but do you know the man? Learn about the life of one of comics' most influential artists and one of the founding fathers of Marvel. See rare sketches and classic comics pages in this comprehensive pictorial history of "The King."

The Art of Will Eisner. Will Eisner. Princeton, Wisconsin; Kitchen Sink Press, 1982. With his prototype superhero character, *The Spirit*, Eisner created a potent world of unparalleled comics storytelling. Learn about the man, his early creations, and his signature approach to comics, which continues to inspire new generations of artists. Note: Also available are Eisner's graphic novels, including *A Life Force, Invisible People*, and *A Contract with God*.

Tintin and the World of Herge: An Illustrated History. Inspired by the classic American comic strip work of George McManus, Herge created a world for his adventurous character Tintin that is timeless in its imagination and accessible to any age reader. Learn about the man behind the work in this highly recommended pictorial history. Or, escape to fantastic places in countless Tintin comics tales (available separately), such as *The Red Sea Sharks, Explorers on the Moon,* and *Tintin in Tibet.*

Toth, Black and White. Edited by Manuel Auad. San Francisco, California; Auad Publishing, 1999. If you've never heard of *Bravo for Adventure* or the other comics created under the sharp eye of Alex Toth, you don't know what you're missing. Like Noel Sickles or *Terry and Pirate's* Milton Caniff before him, Toth is a master of storytelling through an economy of line, expression, texture, and setting. Even today, few artists have even come close.

Comic Books and Graphic Novels

The Adventures of Sock Monkey. Tony Millionaire. Portland, Oregon; Dark Horse Comics, Inc., 2000. Millionaire's comics chronicle the wide-eyed adventures of a stuffed toy, Sock Monkey, and bird named Mr. Crow. Millionaire is the recipient of the 2001 Eisner Award for best writer/artist.

Bone. Jeff Smith. Cartoon Books, 2001. These award-winning comics are packed with fun, adventure, great characters, and excellent stories. Join adorable Fone Bone and friends as they explore the ancient city of Altheia or get into other general mischief. Also look for *Rose*, by Smith and Charles Vess, a beautifully done spin-off to *Bone*.

Daredevil, the Man Without Fear. Frank Miller and John Romita, Jr. New York, New York; Marvel, 2001. This 160-page book collects the riveting comics that helped make *Daredevil* hugely popular again and give Horn-Head new character depth.

Dexter's Lab. Various. New York, New York; DC Comics, Inc., 2001. Whatever pint-sized scientist Dexter is working on in his lab, you can bet his sister Didi is going to meddle with it. If you enjoy Genndy Tartokovsky's *Dexter* cartoons, try these hilarious comics!

Hero Bear and the Kid. Mike Kunkel. California; The Astonish Factory, 2001. With a surface lovingly reminiscent of *Calvin and Hobbes*, Kunkel's comic follows the delightful all-ages adventures of a kid and his superhero polar bear with a big red cape. It's one of the better comics to recently emerge from a small independent publisher.

Illegal Alien. James Robinson and Phil Elliot. Northampton, Massachusetts; Kitchen Sink Press, Inc., 1995. Before James Robinson created and/or wrote comics such as *Leave It to Chance, Starman*, and *Vigilante*, he teamed with artist Phil Elliot to weave an endearing tale of an alien that comes to Earth, inhabits a human body under circumstances he can't control, and helps fulfill the dreams of the people around him. It's one of the "lost" new classics of comics.

Invisible People. Will Eisner, Northampton, Massachusetts; Kitchen Sink Press, Inc., 1993. Legendary Will Eisner weaves the tales of three pitiable, but inspiring, characters, all but anonymous in urban sprawl. Once again, we see Eisner's motif of identity in city life handled with typical mastery.

Krazy and Ignatz: The Komplete Kat Komics. George Herriman. Forestville, California; Turtle Island/Eclipse Books, circa 1990. A cat. A mouse. A brick. A simple formula for story made classic in the hands of an American master. The power of the work has not lost its luster since first produced in the early twentieth century. As with Walt Kelly's *Pogo*, the quirky narrative voice transports the reader directly into a vibrant time and landscape long since past.

Magic Whistle. Sam Henderson. Alternative Comics, 2001. Sam's deceptively simple art is a popular mainstay in *Nickelodeon Magazine.* You can read whole issues of his signature brand of humor. This comic is especially inspiring to new comics artists.

Monkey vs. Robot. James Kochalka. Portland, Oregon; Top Shelf, 2000. Whether you just love comics or just love monkeys and robots, this book has what you need! The creator of *Magic Boy and Girlfriend* and *Peanutbutter and Jeremy* shows you the riotous, age-old feud between the two protagonists. Kochalka's vision and broad style is instantly accessible . . . and contagious!

Mutts. Patrick McDonnell. Kansas City, Kansas; Andrews McMeel, 2000. Rarely does a comic strip like *Mutts* come along that takes the best cues from magical strips like *Pogo, Krazy and Ignatz, Peanuts,* and *The Kinderkids,* to weave a modern classic. Somehow a simple strip about two dog pals becomes a transcendent allegory. If you're not already under its spell, check out various collections, including *Mutts 2: Cats and Dogs, Mutts 3: More Shtuff,* and *Mutts 6: A Little Look-See.*

Out There. Brian Augustyn and Humberto Ramos. La Jolla, California; Wildstorm, 2001. There're some weird things going on in E-D City; and Zach, Casey, Mark, and Jess are smack in the middle of it. Are "ordinary" teens the only defense against the Dreadrealm? The creator of *Crimson* returns with typical quality in this comic series.

Pastille. Francesca Ghermandi. France; Editions du Seuil, 2001. This wordless graphic novel by French artist Ghermandi is indescribably good. Join Pastille, a little girl with a head shaped like a big aspirin, as she turns the mundane into the exciting and the exciting into the unbelievable. It's one of the finest new examples of acute comics storytelling.

Powerpuff Girls. Various. New York, New York; DC Comics, Inc., 2001. Join Buttercup, Blossom, and Bubbles, the supergirl heroes of Townsville, as they battle brainy chimp Mojo Jojo, the devilish Him, and other meanies. Also, if you navigate through the cartoonnetwork.com web site, you'll find *Powerpuff Girls* sketches and model sheets, which can help your own comics.

Ranma 1/2. Rumiko Takahashi. San Francisco, California; Viz Communications, 2001. During a trip to China, Ranma Saotome hits some bad luck and falls into a cursed well where a woman drowned. Now, anytime he's dowsed with cold water, he changes into a female version of himself, while warm water changes him back . . . always at the worst time! What's more, his father ran into a curse, too, and now changes into a panda! Several square-bound volumes of this delightful all-ages manga are available.

The Remarkable Worlds of Professor Phineas B. Fuddle. Boaz and Erez Yakin. New York, New York; Paradox Press DC, 2001. When a wacky British scientist uses his time machine to "improve" the past, his good intentions undo the natural course of the cosmos. Available as a comic series and a collection.

Ultimate Spider-Man. Brian Michael Bendis and Mark Bagley. New York, New York; Marvel, 2001. The writer and co-creator of *Powers, A.K.A. Goldfish*, and *Jinx* is also the guy tapped to breathe vibrant new life into ol' Webhead! Don't miss his exciting, unpredictable take on Marvel's flagship character.

Note: For even *more* great comics and graphic novels, see what's contained in the artist profiles throughout this book.

Magazines

Nickelodeon Magazine. 1633 Broadway, New York, New York; 10019. www.nick.com The comics section of *Nickelodeon Magazine* is typical stomping ground for some of comics' best creators, including Sam Henderson, Mark Martin, and Craig Thompson. You can always count on funny, clever stuff. It's great inspiration as you start your own comics.

Sketch Magazine. Blue Line Productions, 8385 U.S. Highway 42, Florence, Kentucky 41042. www.blpcomics.com. Each issue of *Sketch* offers extensive how-to advice on refining your pencils, inks, writing, coloring, and creating your own comics, *and* has a featured creator, so you can learn from your favorite artist.

Wizard, the Comics Magazine. Wizard Entertainment, 151 Wells Avenue, Congers, New York 10920-2064. www.wizardschool.com. Aside from news, information, and fun features concerning your favorite comics, *Wizard* offers how-to sections where pro artists offer you tips they've learned along the way. If you go to the web site address above, you can learn more about their "school," an on-line place to submit your work and have it reviewed by established artists, editors, and publishers.

Art Contests

AmazingKids! You can send your comics to *AmazingKids!* and they'll display them in their AK Comics section! Check out their web site and find out more information before sending at http://www.amazing-kids.org.

The Refrigerator Art Contest. Each week the producers of the Refrigerator Art Contest pick five pictures to display in "The Competition." Then web site viewers from around the globe vote on their favorite piece of art. If you're the lucky winner, your picture is posted on the web site for one week and then onto "The Hall of Fame" to stay on the fridge for good. For an entry form and rules, click onto http://www.artcontest.com.

Arts and Kids Annual Open Art Competition. Every year "Arts and Kids" accepts entries for its Annual Open Art Competition. The contest is open to anyone under the age of seventeen. You can send one piece of original work of art, in any style or any mediums. http://www.artsandkids.com/Contest/artcontest.asp.

Kidsbookshelf.com You can send in your artwork to be posted on this cool web site! Find out more about it at http://kidsbookshelf.com.

Art Schools

If you decide to go to art school for comics, you want to make sure that they offer either an accredited program or classes in sequential art or illustration. The schools below offer at least one or the other, as well as courses in art history, sculpture, animation, and video game design. Check out their web sites or order an admissions catalog for more info.

Academy of Art College, http://www.academyart.edu

Art Academy of Los Angeles (Sherman Oaks), http://www.associatesinart.com

Kubert School, http://www.joekubert.com

Pasadena Arts Center College, http://www.artcenter.edu

Savannah College of Art and Design, http://www.scad.edu

Parsons, http://www.parsons.edu

Rhode Island School of Design, http://www.risd.edu

School of Visual Arts, http://www.schoolofvisualarts.edu

Comics Company Web Sites

Dark Horse Comics

The publisher of *Hellboy, SpyBoy, Star Wars, Buffy the Vampire Slayer, Planet of the Apes, Sock Monkey*, and others. http://www.darkhorsecomics.com

DC Comics

The publisher of *Batman, Superman, Justice League, Young Justice, Green Arrow, Starman, Powerpuff Girls,* and others. They publish more comics under these banners: Wildstorm *(Gen13)*, Paradox *(Phineas B. Fuddle)*, and Vertigo *(Hellblazer)*. http://www.dccomics.com

Marvel Comics

The publisher of *Spider-Man, Iron-Man, The Hulk, The X-Men, The Avengers, Thor, The Fantastic Four, Daredevil,* and others. http://www.marvelcomics.com

Oni Press

The publisher of *Blue Monday, The Coffin, Magic Pickle, Volcanic Revolver, Whiteout, Grrl Scouts,* and others. http://www.onipress.com

PlanetLar

The publisher of *Foot Soldiers, Astronauts in Trouble, Channel Zero, Sky Ape,* and others. http://www.ait-planetlar.com

Top Cow Productions

The publisher of *Witchblade, Fathom, The Darkness, Tomb Raider, Aphrodite IX,* and others. http://www.topcow.com

Top Shelf

The publisher of *Goodbye, Chunky Rice*; *Monkey vs. Robot*; and other works by James Kochalka; *Hutch Owens* by Tom Hart, and others. http://www.topshelfcomix.com

Xeric Foundation

This foundation has provided monetary grants to comics works such as *King of Persia* and *Pablo's Inferno*, among others. See their web site for a complete list of past winners and guidelines on submitting work for grant consideration. http://www.artcomic.com/xeric.html

Comics Convention Web Sites

Alternative Press Expo (APE), San Francisco; **WonderCon,** Oakland; and **Comic-Con International**, San Diego. http://www.comic-con.org

Dragon-Con, Atlanta, http://www.dragoncon.org

Pittsburgh Comic-Con,
http://www.pittsburghcomicon.com

Small Press Expo, Maryland, http://www.spxpo.com

Wizard World, Chicago, http://www.wizardworld.com

Essential Comic Book Terminology

Now that you're familiar with most of the terms covered throughout the book, here are a few more, so you'll *really* know your stuff!

Anime [annie-MAY]: The Japanese word for animation. A widely popular style of Japanese animation, similar to the American cartoon, but having its own singular style and a wide range of subject matter.

Background: The setting of a story when it is actually drawn onto the comics page.

Balloons: The flat bubble-like spaces with ovals with hooks or "tails" that contain the words the characters are speaking.

Bleed: A stylistic choice used by the artist to fill up the gutter, or white space around the panels, with art,. Bleed art goes right to the edge of the page.

Character: A fictional person or creature portrayed in your comic, whom the story is based around.

Comic book: A sequence of art and words that tell a story and are typically bound into book or magazine form.

Comic strip: A series of art and words in short, horizontal format, generally three to eight panels.

Credits: The acknowledgement of the creative staff of a comic book, which is usually done by listing their names and respective job next to the creator's name.

Graphic novel: A novel written in comic book format, usually 100 pages or more, with a square binding.

Gutter: A thin strip of blank white space that runs between individual panels.

Inker: An artist who goes over the penciled page of comics art with a brush or ink quill to enhance reproduction.

Letterer: A person who draws all the words of dialogue and sound effects in a comic book.

Manga (mahn-GAH): The Japanese word for comic book or graphic novel, which is used in English to describe Japanese comic books or a style of comics art.

Panel: The blocks of art, usually framed, that make up a comic strip or book.

Penciler: An artist who draws a comic book only in pencil.

Printing: The process of producing printed material by ink or press. Printing takes original comic book art to its published comic book form.

Spine (binding): The folded or hinged back of a book that holds its pages together. A spine can be stapled, sewn, or glued.

Title: Also known as a header or logo, the title is the name of a comic book. The logo is another name for the title in its official, designed form.

Theme: The underlying subtext behind the telling of a story.

Writer: A person who writes the script that a comic book artist follows when drawing the pages.

About the Author

Phil Amara began reading comics at a young age, the first titles being *Donald Duck* and *Robot Fighter*. His all-time favorites include Will Eisner's *The Spirit*, Winsor McCay's *Little Nemo in Slumberland*, Marshall Rogers' *Batman*, and Michael Golden's *Micronauts*. In college, he produced a radio show, *Comics Close-up*, and interviewed such greats as Stan Lee, Moebius, and the late Jack Kirby. He has written articles on comics for *Comics Buyers' Guide*, *Comics Scene*, and the Boston *Tab*. He's received his M.A. in business from Emerson College, but more important-ly, is a huge fan of the Adam West *Batman* TV series. Amara is the co-creator of *Burglar Girls, The Nevermen*, and *Sky Ape*, and has written for *Star Wars* and *Aliens*, among others. He is currently the editor on *SpyBoy, Planet of the Apes*, and the Eisner Award-winning *Sock Monkey*, as well as coeditor on the American Illustration Award-winner, *Scatterbrain*, all for Dark Horse Comics. His new favorite comic is *Mia* by Enrico Casarosa.